RESURGENCE
Revitalising Western Catholicism –
An Australian Response

Resurgence

Revitalising Western Catholicism – An Australian Response

James Grant OLSC

Modotti Press

Connor Court Publishing Pty Ltd

Copyright © James Grant 2014

ALL RIGHTS RESERVED. This book contains material protected under International and Federal Copyright Laws and Treaties. Any unauthorised reprint or use of this material is prohibited. No part of this book may be reproduced or transmitted in any form or by any means, electronic or mechanical, including photocopying, recording, or by any information storage and retrieval system without express written permission from the publisher.

PO Box 224W
Ballarat VIC 3350
sales@connorcourt.com
www.connorcourt.com

ISBN: 9781925138412 (pbk.)

Cover design by Blue Vapours

Printed in Australia

Dedicated to Dolores, Audrey, Jessica and Glenn

A special thanks to Richard Alston for his support
and interest in all my work

In grateful remembrance of:

Mary Wood
Fr Neville McKie
Nicholas Wésen

Who have all given me so much

CONTENTS

About the Author viii

Foreword by Richard Alston x

1 The State of Play in the Western World 1

2 What's So Special about Catholicism Anyway 23

3 What Works and What Doesn't – A Snapshot of the Catholic Church beyond Australia 27

4 Catholicity and Western Culture – The Historical Truth of Catholic Centrality to Western civilisation 46

5 Catholicism and the West – National Socialism, Communists and Secularism 60

6 The Struggle for Jesus – Catholic and Islamic Interpretations 71

7 Catholicism and Beauty 78

8 Catholicism and the Economy 86

9 The Greens Political Movement 102

10 Catholicism and Australian Culture – Bogans: A Permanent Australian Underclass? 119

11 Free Will: Chaos or Control? 129

12 Catholicism and Government 134

13 A Confident Catholic Future 141

14 What's To Be Done – Three Achievable Initiatives 153

About the Author

Fr James Grant OLSC (MAICD BA, BTh, GDip IS, GDip Comp ST, GDip Trauma Counselling) was born in Adelaide and schooled in Essendon, Victoria. Fr James joined the Commonwealth Police in 1977 with an initial posting in Canberra. He has qualified as a martial arts instructor in Brazilian Jiu Jitsu, scuba diving and played first grade cricket for Northcote.

Fr James undertook theological studies at Melbourne University, graduating in 1984. Appointed to the UK as an associate priest, He became one of London's first white vicars to minister to the expanding West Indian community Fr James initiated his first interfaith gatherings in west London following the Brixton riots, after which he was appointed on short term placement to Berlin (West Germany) in 1988 and Budapest in 1989.

Fr James returned to Australia in 1989 where he was Senior Chaplain at Geelong Grammar School for seven years, followed by two years at St Michael's Grammar and six years at The Peninsula School. He was noted for his pastoral care with a focus on martial arts, football and cricket as methods for building confidence in students.

In 2004 he was appointed a parish priest at St Stephen's, Richmond, then in 2005 Melbourne's first team vicar for the new parish of Jika Jika in Melbourne's north with responsibility for a large Sudanese refugee community. As parish priest for the Preston area, he was a strong advocate for the Nuba people of Sudan, who are experiencing genocide. He has built two schools in Northern India.

Fr James founded Chaplains Without Borders in 2004 to initiate new ventures into corporate and community organisations, and CWB grew to be Australia's largest chaplaincy service within two years. He went on to be appointed as the world's first chaplain to the casino industry in 2006 (Crown Enterprises Australia), a position he still retains.

As a leading traditionalist within the Australian church, Fr James supported the development to the Anglican Ordinariate in Australia and served on the national committee as secretary 2010-2011. He was received into the Catholic Church and ordained as a Catholic priest in September 2012 as a foundational priest for the Australian Ordinariate. In 2012 he was appointed National Director for Ordinariate schools and to the Ordinariate governing council.

Fr James has continued to develop missions including Catholics in Business 2012 and Catholics in Mission and Renewal in 2013. His CYA (Catholic Youth Academy) youth program works through Crown Casino to develop confidence in de-motivated young Australians and find work placements within Crown. In 2013 he co-established the Renewal Centre. He is married to Dolores and has a daughter Jessica.

He is the first chaplain appointed to an A League soccer club in Australia at the largest Australian club, Melbourne Victory.

Web: www.chaplainswithoutborders.org; www.catholicsinbusiness.org; www.thecyaproject.org; www.renewalcentre.com.au; www.theresurgence.org.

Foreword

The world currently seems a very turbulent place. But it has probably always been so, as people are always apprehensive about the future, which by definition is unknown. Even as far back as the fourth century, in the time of St Augustine, there was chaos and uncertainty all around – the Roman Empire was crumbling and Christianity was taking root as the official religion. It was a time of great political stress and widespread religious anxiety, but people had their religion to comfort and sustain them. Despite the emergence of Islam in the seventh century, the Eastern Orthodox schisms, the subsequent Crusades and the endless wars on the European mainland, the Christian faith was the rock on which Western society rested.

This all changed with the Reformation, the Renaissance and the Enlightenment, but it was not until the 20th century and the rise of the evil trilogy of Communism, Fascism and Nazism, that widespread disillusionment set into many Western societies. Hilaire Belloc defines paganism as the absence of the Christian revelation. Writing in 1931 he said presciently: "It must be evident to everybody by this time that, with the attack on Faith and the Church at the Reformation, the successful rebellion of so many and their secession from United Christendom, there began a process which could only end in the complete loss of all Catholic doctrine and morals by the deserters."

This has occurred over time as "progressive" writers have contradicted and opposed the old inherited Christian system of morals to which people used to adhere long after they had given up definite doctrine. In *The Quest for God*, the eminent historian Paul Johnson maintains that the decline of belief in Natural Law has been accompanied by the growth of moral relativism, which he regards as the cardinal sin of the 20th century, the reason why it has been such a desperately unhappy and destructive epoch in human history. It teaches that axioms of right or wrong vary according to time and place and custom: there are no absolutes, merely the norms of particular societies. In earlier times this would have been seen as a heresy, albeit not an internally valid one, as those who profess to accept its lack of any moral absolutes in practice still regard certain crimes, such as theft and murder as beyond the pale. Johnson sees this as evidence of conscience, not accidentally acquired but an intrinsic part of the divine scheme. The great evil philosophies of the century, Nazism and Communism, were morally relativistic; they argued that the "Revolutionary Conscience" or " the higher law of the Party" were superior to the ancient prescriptive moral wisdom of humanity.

Europeans now live in an age of pervasive secularism and increasing spiritual apathy, beset by false gods such as aggressive atheism, moral relativism and assertive humanism. Equality and non-discrimination are the buzz words, often accompanied by a desire to squeeze religion out of the public square. This lethal combination has not yet hit Australian shores, but we are heading in the same direction, unless religion can regain its confidence and make an attractive offering to its adherents and the wider community.

This is a very timely book, as it addresses not only why there is a deepening moral abyss in this country, but also considers what Australia needs to do to avoid the pitfalls of other Western countries. Unlike many armchair theorists or disheartened clerics, the author has spent a lifetime at the coal face. He is therefore uniquely placed to understand why many denominations seek the wrong zeitgeist solutions to the religious inertia, apathy and disinterest which are threatening to overwhelm both churches and communities.

Fr James Grant is a very unusual cleric, having followed in the footsteps of John Henry Newman as a convert from Anglicanism to Catholicism. He has a clear-eyed view, based on firsthand experience in the field, of why the Anglican Church is crumbling into irrelevance.

Its capture, by those who see social justice as its lodestone, has resulted in an ever increasing effort to "improve" society by responding to the contemporary political mood, usually followed by calls to spend ever more on endless worthy causes. The great Catholic public advocate Fulton Sheen in his popular work, *Peace of Soul* (1950), argued that the attraction of social Christianity for those who seek to have the church pursue worthy causes is that this kind of religion is very comfortable because it leaves the individual conscience alone. Sheen diagnosed the prevailing moral decline thus: "The modern soul no longer looks to find God in nature." How surprised he would be, little more than half a century later, to find that nature has become a substitute religion for many.

The end result is that this concentration on the material world is at the expense of the spiritual, leaving the clientele feeling neglected and marginalised. It is clear that there is something wrong when, in an era of unparalleled affluence, signs of social dysfunction are everywhere – obesity, drug taking, alcohol abuse and family breakdown. Most able bodied citizens have it within their grasp to lead healthy, satisfying and productive lives – instead many spend countless hours watching mindless reality television or whiling away their hours on personal devices.

No longer forced to eke out a marginal living, the ordinary middle of the road Australian has succumbed to the rising affluence of the age and is content to pursue materialistic goals. This is despite the fact that they do not bring inner happiness, but rather social apathy and an inner emptiness. We seek to be saved but in our own way, not God's. Very often we hear people assert that we should be free to worship God, each in our own way. Like those who claim that they have a spiritual rather than a religious impulse, this is little more than the sin of pride – we don't need God because we know better than He does.

As the renowned psychoanalyst Erich Fromm points out in his

1976, *To Have or to Be*: "The achievement of wealth and comfort for all was supposed to result in unrestricted happiness for all." Throw in unlimited freedom and a new religion of Progress was to replace the City of God. But as he wisely points out, unrestricted satisfaction of all desires is not conducive to well-being, nor is it the way to happiness, or even to maximum pleasure. The older we get the more we realise that bodily self-control is the key to physical health, and the same can be said for spiritual contentment.

The great Masters drew the distinction between purely subjectively felt needs, or desires, whose satisfaction leads to monetary and material pleasures, and objectively valid needs – those rooted in human nature and whose realisation is conducive to human growth and well-being.

We are fortunate that it is not yet ten years since the death of one of the towering giants of the Church, John Paul II. This charismatic, indefatigable and practical intellectual sought to turn unbelievers away from "dishonourable living" by promoting an ethos of sacrifice and a national moral renewal based on service to others.

His country of birth, Poland, stands as a beacon of Catholicism, with the highest proportion of church goers in the world – if they can do it, why not us?

Founded in the 13th century by St Dominic to preach the Gospel and to combat heresy, the teaching activity of the Dominicans, the Order of Preachers and its scholastic organisation placed them in the forefront of the intellectual life of the Middle Ages.

Perhaps even more significant, given its pivotal role in arresting the Reformation, was the formation of the Jesuits – an elite religious community of high intellect, great spiritual commitment and a strong sense of discipline.

How can we follow in the footsteps of these great orders? Do we lack Church leaders of stature ready and able to hold their own in debate in the public square?

The Second Vatican Council (1962-65) was an attempt to focus on the problems of the contemporary world, and especially the crisis of humanism – an opportunity to define the human condition and respond to the genuine needs of its members. John Paul II saw it as a time of "great spiritual enrichment", thanks to worldwide community input, and so important that he attended every session.

Critically, the Council saw its role as one of delivering persuasive arguments rather than moralisation and exhortation. John Paul II embraced a dialogue with atheism which did not get bogged down in trying to prove the existence of God, but rather engaged in a conversation about discovering the human person's "interior liberty".

As George Weigel argues in his monumental work, *Witness to Hope*, to defend these truths is not be doctrinaire but rather to be doctrinally serious. The Catholic Church has its bodies of truth, but they have boundaries – it can be flexible, but not infinitely plastic. As John Paul II told UNESCO in 1980, a growing lack of confidence about humanity's prospects was draining modern life of the "affirmation and joy" essential to human creativity. This required a spiritual response to the religious impulse in all of us.

In his encyclical *Laborem Exercens* (On Human Work), this great Pope taught that, through work, men and women participate "in the very action of the Creator of the universe". Work is not only a "good thing" for us all, but it enables our fulfillment as human beings.

This being so it could be expected that church advocates for low income earners would be keen to be involved in debates about how to expand the jobs-generating small business sector, instead of simply arguing for higher welfare payments as the solution to unemployment.

Noel Pearson has transformed the policy debate in indigenous communities by arguing that "welfare is killing my people", displaying an acute understanding of the demoralisation of generations of families on long term welfare. There is surely a wider lesson to be learnt.

As John Paul II has argued, poverty in the modern world is primarily a matter of exclusion from the world of productivity and exchange. We should think of the poor in terms of their potential, and justice demands that their potential be given the opportunity to fulfill itself. Welfare systems that promoted dependency were clearly excluded by such a moral principle. An understanding of economics, with all its shortcomings, is urgently needed for intra church debate.

To those who believe that the Church has "outgrown" evangelism and should concentrate its efforts on social change, the Pope replied that the Church ceases to be relevant when it ceases to preach Jesus Christ. He would make priestly training more rigorous by stressing the centrality of spiritual formation and a demanding academic formation in philosophy and theology. He argued that in many countries priests serve the most well-educated laity in the history of Christianity. Priests who lack intellectual maturity and an ongoing interest in theology will not be able to make the Gospel credible to the legitimate demands of human reason.

Perhaps the fact is that, like the aristocracy of olden times, today's clergy have an instinctive disdain for commerce and all its trappings. As a result they have no understanding of the basic principles which drive our modern economies. How many have ever thought about, let alone read, Adam Smith. As a result they either wallow in cheap shots of social criticism, a field in which everyone is an expert or simply turn off and seek other solaces. Such an assessment could go some way to explaining the unforgiveable descent of priests who have fallen into the terrible sin of sexual abuse of minors.

One of the key messages of the Old Testament was to divest oneself of all unnecessary material possessions. But while most –

then and now – regard this as an unrealistic aspiration, and not to be taken literally, the desert fathers certainly did not, and many were attracted to their example. Fr Grant's insights suggest that people still have an instinctive yearning for the non-material, but they are bereft of spiritual guidance from those equipped to provide it at the local level.

However, all is not lost. Despite it being a central tenet of the French Enlightenment that modernity would kill religion, statistics about religious observance seem to indicate that, outside Europe, this is not so. Currently three-quarters of the global population acknowledge adherence to one of the world's four biggest religions – Christianity, Islam, Buddhism and Hinduism.

For most casual observers the revival of religion means the revival of Islam, but Christianity is also growing rapidly, especially in emerging economies. In 1900 there were roughly 10 million Christians in Africa – a hundred years later the number is over 400 million. In Latin America, long nominally Catholic, evangelical faiths are giving it a real run for its money. Today there at least 500 million revivalists, such as Pentecostalists, around the world. *God is Back*, a recent book by two writers for *The Economist*, argues that in affluent America God and Mammon often appear to have entered into a joint venture to deliver personal happiness and success. While traditional faiths like the Episcopalian Church have been in free fall, Southern Baptists have prospered. In Australia, Hillsong, a Pentecostal mega church has been thriving, while traditional Christian churches such as Methodists and Presbyterians have been subsumed or disappeared.

However, there are many ways of skinning a cat. The leading Anglican philosopher Roger Scruton says that the desire for sacrifice is rooted deep in all of us, best exemplified by the charitable impulse to help others – indeed he quotes Durkheim as regarding it as the core religious experience. The Stoic philosophers of the third to fourth centuries BC Athens believed in Natural Law, expressed in the law of conscience and duty. People are called upon to give their lives in time of war, to sacrifice their present comforts for the sake of their children and to make the daily sacrifice of forgiveness, whereby they renounce vengeance and satisfaction for the sake of others in whom they have no special interest.

Altruism is not just an instinctive thing, it is also a considered response, based sometimes on love of neighbour, sometimes on complex interpersonal emotions like pride and shame, which are in turn founded on the recognition of the other as another like me. Scruton makes the important point that people who are looking for God are not looking for proof of God's existence, but rather for a subject-to-subject encounter which in some way reaches beyond this life.

Religion is a social phenomenon – you don't merely believe a religion, you belong to it – and the individual search for God answers to a deep need of the species. But it also offers a powerful narrative of past events and unseen presences, through which to endow the trivial matter of our species' life with a goal and a meaning. Scruton compares the religious experience to some art forms – music, he suggests, requires us to respond to a subjectivity that lies beyond the world of objects, in a space of its own. Art, literature and the recorded history of mankind tell the story of our religious need, and of our quest for the being who might answer it.

The opportunity is there for churches to fill this yawning gap and provide some food for the soul – rediscovering that human nature is moral and spiritual, not simply material – something the human rights movement is instinctively grasping for: a goal, a purpose in life, a sense of dignity.

Augustine's own spiritual struggles reflected the historical transition from a dying pagan antiquity to the Christian Middle Ages. Just as St Augustine "established anew the ancient Faith", so must we set about the task with urgency, for if we fail to reinvigorate the spirit of the people we are likely to find that we become simply irrelevant, leaving those desperately searching for meaning in their lives as the biggest losers.

Richard Alston

Richard Alston is a former barrister and from 1986 to 2004 he was a Liberal member of the Australian Senate, representing the state of Victoria.

From 1996 to 2003 he was Minister for Communications, Information Technology and the Arts and Deputy Leader of the Government in the Senate.

From 2005 to 2008, he was Australian High Commissioner (Ambassador) to the United Kingdom in London.

1

THE STATE OF PLAY IN MODERN AUSTRALIA

Australian society in the last ten years has revealed a notable degree of angst over the quality of life and community coherence that we currently experience.

Many Australians would point to a deep concern over the quality of our public and private lives. Increases in crime, high prison populations, gangland wars, motorcycle bikie illegality, high rates of depression and suicide, abortion and escalating drug abuse, child abuse all point to downward trends in our general sense of community coherence.

Along with these melodramatic aspects of Australian life is an affiliated uneasiness with the debasement of standards, affecting our education institutions, television, radio and internet, coupled with a lack of general civility and upsurge in coarseness in our society.

As a nation which enjoys significant material wealth, a commitment to democracy and substantial funding to educational and health sectors, this fearfulness and dismay is surprising. If wealth, education, civil peace and democracy are unable to produce a contented society, then what does Australia seem to be missing and what can it do to create a more mutually beneficial and coherent society for all?

It is my contention that Australia needs an overhaul and restoration of its religious dimensions, if it is to again contribute to the provisions of the full life required by its citizens. Yet most importantly, this restoration can only be activated, sustained and brought to fulfilment by the Roman Catholic Church in the Australian context. Significantly, in my view, Catholicism had drawn back from this essential public role, and failed to resist its removal from public life with sufficient vigour.

This series of essays is a call for Australian Catholics to grasp in all its fullness the historical mandate commanded by Christ for the transformation of society and culture alongside its commitment to the health and welfare of the individual.

Certainly, it is easy to argue that turmoil in society and religion always seems worse now than in other generations, yet this is not a call to a return to "golden" past era, for Australia or for Catholicism, but a call to undertake a future not previously attempted.

Australian society and Catholicism now importantly need each other, even if this has not always been the case in the past. There are a number of vacuums in Australian society, around the public domain, that if not filled by "Catholicism" risk leading our nation into a fragmented, incoherent and depressing form of life that could no longer be properly termed a "society" or "community life".

The Yale classics professor Donald Kagan has argued that Western beliefs, ideas and cultural authority are dissolving under the weight of nihilistic philosophies being injected into our educational systems:

> Nihilism rejects any objective basis for society and its morality, the very concept of objectivity, even the possibility of communication itself, and a vulgar form of nihilism has a remarkable influence in our education system today (*Wall Street Journal*, December 1994).

The concern over Western educational institutions with their heightened espousal and advancement of a general permissiveness, pluralism and nihilistic philosophies has also been amplified by the New York psychologist Paul Vitz:

Deconstructionists have powerfully argued that no written text has any fixed meaning, that all interpretation lies in the eyes of the beholder: and thus we see individual moral relativism being advocated at the highest intellectual levels. Values clarification for the kids; deconstruction for graduate students, meanwhile, feminists, gay and lesbian advocates and other minority groups are arguing that all truth (especially morality) is ideological ... At present there is certainly no answer to this social incoherence and it looks like we are headed into a period of disintegration and increasing domestic conflict" (Paul Vitz, *Psychology as Religion*, 1994, p. 167).

Forty years of radically secular education to which a majority of Australians have been subjected have also certainly taken their toll on Australian intellectual life. Catholicism itself has been subjected to social pressures that tend to diminish its "universal" claims surrounding truth and the Christian Revelation. Indeed, Catholicism's major "crime" in the eyes of secularists is its exclusive claim to be relevant for all humans, to be theologically "the truth" and to promote a form of community life that takes precedence over all others. Indeed, a Jesus who boldly proclaims "I am the way, the truth and the life, no-one comes to the father but by me (John 14, 1-6)" is perhaps more disconnected from the Australian mindset than at any time in our national history.

Ironically, these "secular" challenges have not seen any substantial fight back from the Church. In reality, Catholic doctrine is less likely to be promoted to both believers or the wider society in the faint-hearted belief that many of these teachings will be unintelligible to average Australians.

The revelation of the doctrine of the Trinity is perhaps our greatest example of failure to promote, explain or enlighten Catholic beliefs. Certainly, Trinity can be difficult to describe metaphysically, but this is no excuse to neglect its centrality to Catholic life. Trinity has important implications for the formation of the Church and the way we live as Catholics.

At its most basic, the message of the Trinity is that God is a community. Yes, God is one, but a unique Catholic revelation is that God is three personalities as well – Father, Son and Holy Spirit.

That is a huge difference, there and then, from other philosophies. God is a community. Jews, Muslims, Buddhists and secular Australians won't say anything like this; only Catholics say God is a community! Yet underlying this statement are a number of substantial implications. In Trinity we are called to be part of something, we are meant for community, because God is community and we can only attain the fullness of life in community.

This is a radical departure from almost everything that Australian society extols. There are endless media messages promoting individual culture and we are told daily, to think, choose and act for ourselves – "to thine own self be true", create your own life, be your own person, love who you want, end your life the way you want.

The radical clash between two presentations of life could not be more stark yet, perhaps the truth can be seen in what we have created in Australian life. For every drug addict, every alcoholic, every teenage binge drinker, every gambler, every depressed person, there is one thing in common: they all lack community! Forced by our society to be true to ourselves we have become lost, lonely and afraid!

The reality for Catholicism in modern Australia can be portrayed if we ask ourselves a simple question. Where are most Australians to be found? On the whole we can broadly answer, at school, or in the workplace. In both these environments the Catholic Church is far from prevalent. Certainly in schools, the Catholic Church has had substantial success, with around 1,700 schools across the nation. Nevertheless over 1,200 of these schools are primary schools, suggesting that for most Catholic school students their experience of faith within education ends at around 12 years of age. The total number of Australian students in Catholic schools approaches 30 per cent with the majority of these to be found in NSW and Victoria. Naturally, Catholic schools in the ACT, NT, South Australia, Tasmania and Western Australia account for a much smaller proportion of schools, around 20 per cent of the total.

In general Catholic education is significantly reduced in the secondary years and the spread across the nation is also uneven. Nevertheless, Catholic schools play an important role in the development of faith within the Australian education system.

The same is not the case in the workplace, where Catholic influence is almost extinct. Past connections with the union movement, the YCW and the influence of the Democratic Labor Party in politics, have collapsed over the last 30-40 years. While the National Civic Council founded in the 1940s by prominent Catholic layman B.A. Santamaria has maintained a strong Judeo-Christian social value system, the organisation should now be better understood as a think-tank rather than a Catholic political movement. This leaves the Catholic Church without influence either at boardroom level, or within union structure. This is an extremely serious situation for the Church, without regular "touch points" with working Australians, without chaplains in individual workplaces and without ongoing dialogue with industry groups, the Church has no possibility of ensuring its views on Catholic social teaching, its concern for the family and workers, can be articulated in influential forums.

The Catholic Church is in need of greater influence within the Australian political environment, but particularly with Australian workplaces, industry groups and the union movement. Some work has begun with the formation of Chaplains Without Borders (www.chaplainswithoutborders.org) in 2004 and Catholics in Business (www.catholicsinbusiness.org) in 2012, but the role of both these organisations should be extended and supported at a national level.

A comprehensive representation of Australian life and society suggests that Catholicism is under a subtle yet aggressive form of assault and censure from large sections of media with a view to forcing the Church out of the public domain.

Anecdotally, there is substantial evidence that organisations such as the ABC, the Greens Party, gay and lesbian movements, voluntary euthanasia and assisted suicide groups, and extreme socialists all see the weakening of the Church as a significant step in achieving their social and political goals.

Additionally, wider Australian society has accepted a stringent application of the separation of church and state doctrine which now only rewards and permits religious activity within social justice dimensions and the provision of welfare. If this situation remains unchallenged in Australia, the Catholic Church can expect its influence to eventually disappear for most Australians.

Examples of practical irrelevance for Catholics are abundant – undoubtedly Sunday Mass attendance is now mostly seen as a private decision. These Catholics who attend Mass do not experience discrimination, but the public attitude is that such religious devotion is of no more value than another individual's game of golf, taking the kids to Auskick or spending time with the family. All are private decisions, all are individual choices and none is more valuable than another. Assuredly, prejudice against Catholicism is not a public issue, provided that Catholics stay within "agreed" boundaries. Attempts to move faith outside the private domain bring quick criticism for crossing the public/private, church/state philosophy.

There is also a ruinous cost to the Church. Without the capacity to fulfil its historic mandate to transform society and culture for Christ ("Go and make disciples of all nations baptising them in the name of the Father, the Son and the Holy Spirit", (Matt 28) she suffers a loss of energy, drive and conviction. A tacit acceptance to become a "private" organisation weakens all concepts of mission and growth.

Australian society has also changed significantly in its attitude to the celebration of Christian public holidays. Over the last 20 years the influence of both Christmas and Easter (including Good Friday) have diminished considerably. This is evidenced by the increasingly low key or often non-existent public marking of these events. Progressively, most local governments no longer recognise Christmas or at best will provide a rudimentary tree.

Government schools will usually not mention the reason for the "summer holidays" with local governments and other public institutions citing "diversity and tolerance" combined with an unwillingness to cause offence to Australian's non-Christian communities as reasons for not acknowledging these religions holidays.

Within the Melbourne CBD and business district Chinese New Year now has precedence as the most entertaining on the promotions calendar. This is not to criticise the management of any venue, but it is to acknowledge that changing attitudes are witnessed in commercial decisions. It is time Catholics recognised the departure from past attitudes and practices in Australian society. Ironically, there has been no acknowledgement or efforts to resist this new reality. Perhaps, the higher Mass attendances at both Christmas and Easter mask the changing attitudes of the majority of the population. I am confident that a "returning Christmas" to its "public dimension" campaign would elicit a strong response in most Catholics, yet it requires a greater depth of thinking and a willingness to energise communities to appreciate the value of the "public" message of Christmas.

The task of strengthening the public dimensions of Catholicism is not always made easier by the media. Apart from Cardinal Pell there has been few Catholic leaders with any significant media profile. The Cardinal's own forthright views have made him a controversial figure in sections of the Australian media and while there are one or two "court jester" priests, these comic characters have nothing to say on real Catholic issues, apart from criticism of their own Church! Often the Church does try to distribute "press releases" over particular issues but these are largely ignored by mainstream media outlets.

The Church must do more to establish, organise and control its own media. Crumbs from the media table, usually negative ones, cannot suffice for such a significant religious and cultural player in Australian society.

Catholicism has another profound reason for the establishment of its own media: Our current television, radio and internet quality and informational values are often appallingly low. From minimalistic news programs, to mindless comedy shows, to trashy popular reality television or movies, the intellectual and moral content of our media is in a poor state.

While the link between violent television, film and the increase of violence in our homes and streets is tenuous, the normalising of characters who do nothing but drink, swear and chase women, is boring and sets the lowest possible standards for a well-lived life.

Catholicism has a strong stake in ensuring that its support for the family is underlined. High Australian divorce rates (50 per cent at present) the poverty of single parents and the social costs that arise from these situations should not become even more normative through encouraging presentations in the media.

To an increasing extent, a wide-range of societal problems in Australia can be connected to the increase of family breakdown. It is not a case of apportioning blame to individuals, yet Catholicism has a central role to play in the alleviation of the suffering caused by divorce, family separation and the pain endured and carried for years in our high abortion statistics. Nevertheless, the voice of the Church on these important matters often seems irrelevant to media and government bodies. Indeed mainstream agencies seem to have minimal willingness to fully understand these increasing trends or to provide preventative solutions.

In June 2012, there were 961,000 single parent families in Australia or 15 per cent of the total number, of which 67 per cent had dependent children still at home. Statistics on Australian abortion rates are difficult to obtain as most states and territories do not keep these. Nevertheless general ballpark estimates based on Medicare data suggest a figure of around 80,000 per year. These statistics mask a great deal of pain for individuals, but also suggest ongoing difficulties for Australian society with educational and social welfare provisions continuing to rise.

The huge problems these families experience is at the heart of Catholicism, with Catholicism continually pushed into the private sphere we will continue to see a disconnection between society and the needs of families. If Catholicism has a diminished voice and influence on the Australian family, governments are likely to continue to increase welfare spending while allowing child abuse, mental illness, single parent and divorce rates to continue to rise.

Concurrent with this increasing need for greater attention to the family, regrettably Catholicism and society are witnessing the decline and extinction of the Australian protestant churches. Catholicism needs to be honest and clear about this: in its Australian context there will be no significant assistance or support from the Anglican, Uniting or smaller protestant groups in the struggle to remedy Australian society.

The Anglican Diocesan Financial Advisory Group (DFAG) reported in November 2013:

> The financial health of the Anglican Church, outside the large metropolitan diocese, appears to be in a parlous state. What's more, in light of relevant trends in population shift and declining church memberships, it is hard to see how many dioceses will remain sustainable into the near future.

DFAG went on to mention that six dioceses (of a total of 23

Australia-wide) were recognised by their own registrars as not being financially viable and that another three were in serious financial circumstances.

Arising from this, some hard truths need to be recognised. From the Catholic perspective recent moves to support women's ordination and to condone homosexual clergy who regularly share vicarages as public couples in many dioceses raise questions regarding the catholicity of Anglican practice. Still, perhaps the greatest criticisms have come from within. The 2001 Anglican Constitution Review Commission noted:

> There is at present perhaps a greater fear of each other than has existed for many years. Perhaps it is the case that, as we get poorer, we get more frightened, the more frightened we get, the narrower and meaner and bitter and less secure we are. At present, the church's work cannot go forward and our fears of the past mean we have limited opportunities for change and advancement (Report to General Synod 2001 Book 4B, p. 10).

In coming years Anglicanism will find itself functioning only at very low levels and only in some major capitals. The Uniting Church faces a similar reality. In 2013, the church was forced to sell $53.9 million in assets to recover debts from the collapse of Acacia College and congregations in Tasmania and Victoria were asked to identify surplus properties. While the Uniting Church doesn't have the same difficulties as the Anglicans, they also have experienced a dramatic decline in membership, losing around seven per cent of its membership from the previous census of 2007.

A substantial reason for Anglican and Uniting Church decline is their failure to retain and nurture young people and families. The state of Anglican schools is appalling. In my own 15 years as an Anglican chaplain, students that I instructed made up half of all diocesan confirmations. In my final chaplaincy year over 100 were confirmed of a total diocesan number of 180 for all Anglican schools. The Melbourne Anglican system of 16 schools, regrettably has little concept of sacramental life, subsequently failing to sustain any interest in the faith for young people.

Another alarming feature of the Anglican and Uniting churches is their high numbers of members of retirement age. Melbourne, a larger Anglican diocese, has only around 8,500 regular attendees, with congregation sizes approximately 30 to 50 per week.

Such a collapse of core attendance must stand as a warning to Catholicism. In coming years Catholics must ensure that their missionary activity is attentive to the needs of young families and teenagers. Missionary activity is at the heart of Catholicism yet as the collapse of Anglicanism and other protestant groups clearly shows, an internal focus and the promotion of social agendas within a church will quickly erode the energy, courage and confidence to perform such a mission. Social agendas come in many guises and from my own recollections of Anglican conflicts perhaps the most destructive is "inclusive language". This results in music and liturgy producing unsingable hymns and incomprehensible prayers to our mother and father! It is not without reason these churches are empty. They have failed to maintain the Catholic and Apostolic faith.

The Catholic Church in Australia must be involved in the public domain and continue to speak clearly on issues that concern it. However, as the collapse of the protestant churches demonstrates, this can only be achieved from within the universal Catholic and Apostolic faith. Social agendas not coming from within an Apostolic strand may begin as "support and equality" for women but soon end up with female priests handing out condoms during Easter services and teaching that Jesus has given us the freedom to have sex in whatever form we like (as has already occurred in the USA). Support for the environment may be an important issue, but Anglican services that refer to Mother God and making the sign of the cross with dirt are no longer Catholic in nature.

The ecumenical movement in Australia has reached a crisis point, especially from a Catholic perspective. The changes within the protestant groups now effectively make them difficult to differentiate from wider secular Australia. Most protestants have not reacted to the changes affecting families, to issues of single parents, to the impact of abortions. Indeed unless Catholicism wishes to comment on refugees, or environmental issues, there is in reality no support from amongst the other denominations.

Moreover, there is another significant inducement for Catholics to be cautious in their connection to the ecumenical movement. Importantly, it is only Catholicism that has maintained and expressed an adherence to Apostolic truth, especially the notion that the Church was founded by Jesus Christ to be the vehicle for the salvation of humanity. This doctrine is viewed by protestants as rather quaint, peculiar and not appropriate for today's modern world. Indeed protestant groups have gone much further, propounding the notion that no one faith has all the answers but that all have equal degrees of perfection. Hence tolerance, equality and cooperation have replaced a quest for truth.

Arguments against the Catholic standpoint (that the Church continues the fullness of Christ's revelation, healing and salvation) usually rest on the proposition that the need for peace and tolerance must outweigh claims of religious "superiority" occasionally asserted by Catholics. The ecumenical movement has as a primary supposition "that what we hold in common is more important than that which divides us".

This is no longer true in Australia, nor is it honourable for Catholics to continue to ascribe to protestant groups belief systems they no longer share. Certainly, protestant Christians do speak of strong notions of God's action in the World, but too many liberal protestants no longer see Jesus as God's son, view Mary's virginity, assumption and role in salvation as "unenlightened" and see claims of papal authority as irrelevant. Having removed or downplayed essential doctrines of the faith, it is not surprising that social outcomes such as abortion and gay marriage are advocated on grounds of "equality" or "rights" platforms rather than moral or religious issues.

The ecumenical movement in Australia rests on a manifesto of "core" and "non-core" beliefs, the resultant outcome is a lowest common denominator program which reflects poorly on all. Ecumenism is often sceptical of key Catholic doctrines, such as the divinity of Christ, the virgin birth and the bodily resurrection of Jesus, and within the moral dimension it is generally tolerant of extra-marital sex, abortion and homosexuality.

The central essence of Catholicism is to be found in mission. There has always been for Catholics a great joy in bringing new Catholics into the fullness of the faith. This fullness has a sacramental dimension, a love of the doctrines of the Church and a devotion to Our Lady.

In most Australian protestant groups forming new Christians is not a priority – indeed the sense of uniqueness is so weak in the Anglican and Uniting churches there is effectively nothing to join. The end result is that many now see all protestant groups as almost the same, therefore allegiance is formed on the basis of services provided (such as young mums and baby health groups). A resultant, convenience and self-service mentality is pervasive in all of Australia's protestant groups.

Australian Catholicism can prosper into the future provided it maintains its Catholic identity. This will require the continual assertion that Catholicism is nothing like Australian protestant groups. To be identified in any way with Australian protestants suggests that all Christians are the same. The dramatic decrease in numbers, the abandonment of Apostolic beliefs, the lack of internal discipline, the total emphasis on social agendas and the failure to undertake mission have witnessed the ruination of Australian protestantism. Catholicism must not be associated with this fundamental failure to uphold the Christian heritage handed down from the Apostles.

Australian Catholicism has been deeply affected and sustained by migrant communities, both post-war, with the Italian communities and more recently with Vietnamese and Filipino migration. It is essential to the Catholic future in Australia that these communities are supported, developed and maintained in the faith. Traditionally these communities have great devotion both to the Mass and to Our Lady. These are in my view, two sides of Catholic truth and identity. It is the spiritual maternity of Mary in regard to all the faithful, stemming from her cooperation in the mysteries of the incarnation, the redemption and the distribution of grace. The devotion of migrant Australians to Mary has much to teach us, not only in ensuring that we come closer to Christ in the Mass, but also guaranteeing that our Catholic and Apostolic faith is protected. There is a compelling spiritual argument that the loss of Mary in protestant theology and practice has left these groups without a foundation on which to build.

The humility of Mary and her patient devotion to her son will be needed by Australian Catholics in another continuing struggle. Secularists and moral liberals will not be withdrawing their campaign against the Church any time soon. This can be evidenced by the continual struggle against the Catholic stance on the right to life. Abortion is a difficult issue for many Australians, yet in reality it is not essentially based on a women's right to choose. Abortion goes much deeper. In a society that emphasises sexual freedom there are bound to be considerable numbers of unwanted pregnancies; these pregnancies are often unwanted by men as well. Naturally, the retention of such pregnancies requires a level of commitment not to be found in casual sex. If male attitudes to sexual freedom and lack of commitment were to change there would be significantly fewer single mothers. At the heart of abortion is our single-minded devotion to freedom in all forms of our lives; this single-mindedness confounds both men and women.

Moreover, moral liberals usually have difficulty with the contention that the foetus is human. This is often avoided by resorting to slogans around a woman's right to choose, or the control of an individual's body belongs exclusively to that individual. The Catholic position is not an extreme one, but it does assume that this complex issue is one that concerns both sexes and that the rights of the unborn are at the heart of all our rights. Catholicism is also in the vanguard of matters concerned with suicide and euthanasia and with the further complexity of doctor-assisted suicide.

The right to suicide is usually based on a standpoint of extreme individual rights. The basic idea states that a person wishing to commit suicide is not inflicting direct harm on anybody else, so on what grounds should moral objection be found? The destruction of life is only his or her own.

The Catholic perspective varies considerably from this totally individualised view. For Catholicism the individual acts within a wider context, one that emphasises loyalty to community, respect of family and the view that life is fundamentally a gift from God for the service of others. In Catholicism, the individual is central, but primarily in his or her vocation and service to others. In the same way that it is impossible to be a full individual if a person is only self-orientated it is also impossible to be a Catholic without reference to Christ's Church. It is entirely valid to be a Buddhist by yourself, under your own tree, in your own backyard. For Catholicism, individuality, personality and love are all formed and shaped in community. In the Catholic view individuals without this formation, nurture and continuous contact are very stilted indeed.

The Catholic understanding of the individual nurtured within a community is both the purpose of humanity, but also our hope in facing the myriad problems of Western society. Catholicism must never tire of forming, rebuilding and advocating for community. In the Church's view the fullness of life is only available in this commitment.

Thomas à Kempis wrote in the *Imitation of Christ*: "Be assured of this, that you must live a dying life. The more completely a man dies to self, the more he begins to live to God." On the same theme Evelyn Underhill quoted the German mystic Meister Eckhard: "When I left myself I found God, when I found myself I lost God." Underhill herself noted: "Our eyes are not in focus for this reality, until they are out of focus to our own petty concerns" (Evelyn Underhill, *The School of Charity: Meditations on the Christian Creed*, London, 1952, p. 88).

The underlying assumptions of modern Australian society are exactly the opposite. Shakespeare's words "To thine own self be true" have been extended to a further belief that all things are possible for humanity. Australia promotes equality, tolerance, mass education and continuous progress, all designed to demonstrate the excellence of humanity.

The Catholic tradition would simply point to the current state of Western society and suggest that faith in the individual has failed to deliver human happiness, contentment or security.

Over the last 400 years, secular political philosophies have manifested a number of differing systems promising human fulfilment without the need of God. Significantly, all of these philosophies have shaped their appearance in the form of faith.

The French Revolution, grounded in Enlightenment thinking, chose to proffer pale alternatives to Christian dogma, festivals, liturgy and saints. The American historian R.R Palmer of Princeton and Yale Universities, an expert on 18th century France, noted:

It was their burning faith in things human, their absolute certainty of being right, their passionate and absorbing devotion to the indivisible republic that was their church (R.R. Palmer, *Twelve Who Ruled: The Year of Terror in the French Revolution*, Princeton, 1970, p. 323).

Unfortunately, faith in humanity does not always lead to the promised land of human fulfilment. The French Revolution gave us Maximilien de Robespierre who maintained order through the terror of the guillotine and a desire for religious change that initiated the "cult of the supreme being". During the festival of supreme being in 1794 one of Robespierre's fellow revolutionaries, Jacques-Alexis Thuriot, remarked: "Look at the bugger, it is not enough for him to be master, he has to be God" (David Andress, *The Terror*, Farrer, Straus and Giroux, New York, 2009, p. 310).

The advent of communism in the early 20th century inaugurated similar terrifying results. The Marxist version in particular sought a classless society in which the full realisation of human freedom could be obtained. Yet in reality Marx unleashed in Russia the most destructive secular religion the world has experienced. British social philosopher Sir Isaiah Berlin said of Marx: "Karl Marx was among the great authoritarian founders of new faiths, ruthless subverters, and innovators who interpret the World in terms of a single, clear, passionately held principle, denouncing and destroying all that conflicts with it" (Isaiah Berlin, *Karl Marx, His Life and Environment*, New York, p. 19).

Stephane Courtois, a French historian and former Marxist, wrote an honest appraisal of the realities of communism in his work *The Black Book of Communism* (1997). The book presents an exposition of the crimes of communism committed through the Communist exercise of power. Courtois estimates these crimes to have been responsible for the deaths of nearly 100 million people.

Perhaps the final word should go to Mikhail Bukunin, the Russian revolutionary anarchist who knew Marx well and often contended with him for influence in the emerging communist political perspective: "Marx does not believe in God but he believes much in himself and makes everyone serve him. His heart is not full of love but of bitterness and he has very little sympathy for the human race" (Quoted in Paul Johnson, *Intellectuals*, 1990, p. 72).

Concomitant with Communism, the early 20th century also suffered considerably from the advance of National Socialism. This secular ideology constructed racial theories based on belief in the existence of a master race, superior to all others.

While National Socialism rejected Marxist concepts of class struggle, it opposed ideas of equality of wealth and property and pursued territorial expansion at the expense of those it deemed racially inferior, particularly Jews, gypsies and Slavs.

National Socialism also borrowed heavily from Catholic notions of a messianic saviour, with Christ replaced by the Fuhrer principle in the figure of Adolf Hitler. National Socialism was aided by some theologians such as Ernst Bergmann who contended that Jesus was not a Jew and that Adolf Hitler was the new messiah. The Nazis frequently used the theological views of the protestant Martin Luther expressed in his work *On the Jews and Their Lies* to advocate for persecution of the Jewish race.

Nazism remained hostile to Catholicism throughout its existence, primarily for its perceived allegiance to a non-Germanic leader in the Pope, but also for its persistent opposition to sterilisation programs initiated by the Nazis for those deemed racially inferior. The Church underwent extensive persecution in Europe from 1933 onwards with thousands of priests arrested and killed for their resistance to National Socialism, including the courageous Bernard Lichtenberg and Maximilian Kolbe. It is estimated that over 8,000 priests were sent to concentration camps with 1,034 dying in Dachau, 300 in Sachsenhausen, 780 in Mauthausen and 5,000 at Buchenwald. These numbers do not include those murdered in their parishes or those who died en-route.

The fall of the Berlin Wall in 1989 substantially confirmed that communism and socialism were largely discredited, both as practical political schema and as philosophical perspectives.

In 1992 Francis Fukuyama, an American political scientist, argued that the spread of liberal democracies and the dominance of free market capitalism signalled the end point of humanity's socio-cultural and economic evolution:

> What we may be witnessing is not just the end of the cold war, or the passing of a particular period of post-war history, but the end of history as such: that is, the end point of mankind's ideological evolution and the universalisation of Western liberal democracy as the final form of human government (Fukuyama, *The End of History*, 1989),

In 2014 Fukuyma updated his hypothesis suggesting that "backsliding in democratic growth and freedom, a deterioration of public service [and] weakened civil institutions" all threatened a period of political decay ("Fukuyama: At the end of history still stands democracy", Wall Street Journal, 6 June 2014).

In my perspective, the current deterioration of Western culture represents a "hollowing out" and corrosion of the vital essence of society. We have in the dominance of the "individual above all" philosophy, and the considerable growth of the "rights" agenda adversaries from within who are as radically hostile to Catholicism and the West as were either communism or National Socialism. Simon Breheny, director of the legal rights project at the Australian Institute of Public Affairs has drawn attention to the extensive growth in demand for both "human rights" and increasing "social privileges":

During his state of the Union address on 11 January 1944, US President Franklin D. Roosevelt proposed a "second Bill of Rights". This new Bill of Rights included rights to employment, a living wage, freedom from unfair competition and monopolies, housing, medical care, education and social security. FDR believed that the original US Bill of Rights had proved inadequate to assure equality in the pursuit of happiness. A similar set of human rights was later included in the 1952 Universal Declaration of Human Rights. The Universal Declaration included rights to employment (Article 23) housing, healthcare and welfare (Article 25) and education (Article 26). Of course, none of these things are actually human rights. At best they are policy aspirations. By definition, human rights exist without the need for policies and programs of government. Universal human rights are not privileges granted by the State but restrictions on what the State can do (S. Breheny, *IPA Review*, November 2013).

Over the past 60 years the reach of human rights has extended further and further into the lives of ordinary Australians, but has recently started to affect the Catholic Church as well, threatening to restrict and inhibit Catholic religious freedom. While it is tempting to see the United Nations as a comically ineffective organisation, particularly in 2011 when it declared a new human right of internet access or in 2013 when noting that Australia's reduction of unemployment benefits violated the fundamental right to receive Centrelink payments.

The introduction of substantial new rights legislation under US President Obama was also a fundamental new challenge to Catholic freedom.

In 2012, the US Secretary of Health and Human Services issued a final rule requiring that all women have access to free preventative services, including contraception, from which religious institutions such as hospitals, universities and charities were not exempt. Catholic teaching against sterilisation, artificial contraception and abortion states that these practices are intrinsically immoral and Catholics cannot be involved in them. This is a radically new position in American law that seeks to require individuals to act against their moral convictions and the teachings of Catholicism.

The result of this legislation is that many Catholic providers of health care have been forced to close, after no longer receiving public funding.

In 2010, Catholic charities in Washington DC, the largest provider of foster care and public adoption services closed after the District of Columbia said the charity was ineligible for funding following its refusal to provide same sex couples with adoption services. As an aside, President Obama has recently described Catholic schools as divisive.

This should serve as a warning to Australian Catholics. When religion becomes privatised and removed from the public domain, attacks on Catholic institutions are not far behind.

A Catholic faith that is privatised only seeks to live half a life. Privatised Catholicism is generally ignored by governments and others because it is treated as a therapeutic tool. Prayer, singing, attending Mass, listening to sermons or receiving counselling from a priest, are all benefits to the individual, and provided they affect no-one else they are not seen as harmful.

Nevertheless, Catholicism is not a private organisation. In fact, by its nature, it seeks to engage in the public arena and embody its faith and beliefs in concrete public institutions like schools and hospitals.

The fundamental work of the Church is public and in my view, Australian Catholics and the wider community are faced with a vital question: "Do we continue to not resist the push to make Australian Catholicism a purely private affair, or are we prepared to project a more robust form of Catholic expression, undertaking our faith practice in all areas of society? My strong contention is that Australia risks being a dramatically diminished society if Australian Catholicism cannot revitalise its tenacity to fulfil Christ's mandate.

Further Reading

Edward Norman, *Secularisation*, Continuum, London, 2002.

Charles Taylor, *A Secular Age*, Harvard University Press, 2007.

2

WHAT'S SO SPECIAL ABOUT CATHOLICISM ANYWAY?

Nothing is more central to the success or failure of Western civilisation than Catholicism. Consequently its diminished existence in Australia's society is a pressing cause of anxiety.

Throughout its history, Catholicism has proved to be far from a conventional faith. It contained a new and startling assertion that God sought to become intimate with and inseparable from humanity by sending his son Jesus to be one of us, a new creation that would be both fully human and fully divine. Such an idea was a radical departure from ancient Greek and Egyptian concepts which sometimes envisioned gods and humans engaging in sexual relations or gods taking human form. In both contexts the essential natures of divinity and humanity were not united. The imperial culture of ancient Rome identified emperors with a divinely sanctioned authority, a concept that can be found asserted by many of history's tyrants including Henry VIII of England, Kaiser Wilhelm II of Germany and even secular rulers such as Adolf Hitler and Joseph Stalin.

The divine humanity found in the incarnation of Christ, his love and suffering for humanity and his empathy for the poor and outsiders is in marked contrast to any human system previously invoked.

Moreover, the radical Catholic claim that God, through Jesus, had reconciled himself to all humans through the death and resurrection of his son has no parallels in human thought.

The reality for Catholics in the practice of this faith is a reversal of human values and a transformation of love away from divine power and into the ideas of a suffering and forgiving God. The earliest Catholics, particularly the apostle Paul, formed these new revelations into a set of teachings that have had a vital impact upon the nature of humanity and its future.

At its heart, Catholicism sees God and humanity moving together in a new and profound way. This "good news" is understood by Catholicism as nothing less than the "divinisation of humanity". As Jesus himself said: "In that day you will realise that I am in my Father, and you are in me, and I am in you. Whoever hears my commands and keeps them is the one who loves me. The one who loves me will be loved by my father, and I too will love them and show myself to them" (John 14, 20-21).

The notion of God and humans in loving intimacy had a huge impact on societies influenced in meaningful ways by Catholicism. Humans now had a new challenge to continually improve themselves. Human potential was centred on a partnership with God and marked a new creation no longer bound by human sin and alienation from God's plan. In practical terms, the individual and his relationship with Christ became the primary bond surpassing allegiance to tribe or family. As Paul comments, "It is no longer I who live but Christ who lives in me" (Galatians, 2:20); "There is neither Jew nor Gentile, neither slave nor free, nor is there male and female, for you are all one in Christ Jesus" (Galatians 3:28). This Christian experience of God marked an important new reality: humanity of all classes, states and genders would now be responsible for their own relationships with God and changed with its nurture and development. We must not underestimate how revolutionary and outrageous this idea was to ancient peoples, or indeed how extreme it still seems to our brothers and sisters in Islam and Judaism. Catholic claims that the Father who created heaven and earth would be interested in a loving relationship with even the least of humanity is still a bridge too far for some. Catholicism today, which highlights a loving personal God, of Father, Son and Holy Spirit, and who displays a desire to break down all barriers between himself and us remains the most profound experience of God's love available to us: "For God so loved the world, that he gave his one and only son, that whoever believes in him should not perish but have eternal life" (John 3:16).

Catholicism is different from every other faith in human experience in that its profoundly practical standpoint not only called for a intellectual change but also provided a path of achieving this unity.

For both Christ and the early evangelists (and church) it was no longer necessary to conform to vigorous religious regulations, dietary or tribal restrictions, nor an hereditary priesthood. With the advent of Christ, Catholics emphasised an adherence to conscience, a judgement or "inner voice that moves people to do good under any circumstances and to avoid evil by all means" (*Youth Catechism*, 295). This new emphasis on a relationship with Jesus, formed in personal connections and strengthened by conscience, gave Catholics a direct path to God and emphasised a new found freedom of action for humanity: "Man has the right to act according to his conscience and in freedom so as personally to make moral decisions" (*Catechism of the Catholic Church*, 1782).

The much neglected Catholic sacrament of penance was instituted by the Church to strengthen this relationship. The forgiveness of sins and the healing of relationships was central to Christ's teachings and has been regarded by the Church as a sign of the advent of God's Kingdom and the coming completed relationship between God and humanity. The enfeeblement of this sacrament in Western societies has greatly weakened the life of the faith for many modern Catholics.

The ministry and energies of Jesus focused a great deal on the outsiders of the society of his time. His healing and teaching were mainly directed to sinners, the sick, prostitutes, foreigners and others who might be termed "outsiders" today.

At the formation of the Church, the Apostles rightly understood that this new emphasis from Jesus entailed a levelling of the human playing field. All people were equally loved by God and were to be nurtured in Christ's love and value.

This Catholic emphasis on "social equality" was a profound change from all that had previously existed in human history. This ground breaking change has often been seen as subversive and extremist by various secular regimes, but remains today a central mark of Catholicism throughout the world. The origin of hospitals, belief in the equality of men and women and support for the disadvantaged or outsiders are all concepts founded within Catholicism. Still today the strongest expression of these values can be found clearly in non-Catholic countries. A fine example can be seen in the work of Mother Teresa of India and the healing and educational work of many other Catholic orders and societies. It is still true that non-Catholic societies are significantly lacking in these basic commitments to equality and the fundamental rights of all members of their societies.

The essence of Catholicism is based on the Incarnation, the unique Catholic idea that God became one of us. This view has seen a new and profound understanding of the value and love from God towards humanity. The Catholic Church has always sought to develop this idea into mutual respect for the freedoms of each person.

Profound issues challenge this central Catholic tenet today, the right to life, abortion, the worthless treatment of many at the end of life in various parts of the world, including Australia, are evidence that the work of the Catholic Church is not yet complete.

3

WHAT WORKS AND WHAT DOESN'T?
A SNAPSHOT OF THE CATHOLIC CHURCH
BEYOND AUSTRALIA

Rouen, France: Reclaiming the Culture

Rouen is the modern day capital of upper Normandy and the historic capital of Normandy. For much of its medieval history (11th-15th centuries), Rouen was one of the Anglo-Norman dynasty capitals that ensured a period of significant prosperity.

Christian churches have been present in Rouen from the fourth century and Rollo, a Norse Viking and founder of the Norman principality, was baptised in Rouen Cathedral in 915 AD.

The extensive history of Christianity in Rouen is not hard to see and the smallish CBD contains some six parish churches of cathedral size, along with another eight parish chapels.

Yet, despite this historic Christian strength, the city is largely secularised with these Christian communities only hosting miniscule numbers of practising Catholics. The cathedral and the significant sized abbey of Saint Ouen and Saint Maclou, and the city chapels are largely empty of parishioners. Indeed some have succumbed to the temptation to incorporate modern art displays as a means of attracting visitors.

These Rouen churches immortalised by Monet are stunning to visit, with most largely consisting of high gothic nave, transept and chapels, so their awe inspiring nature is hard to miss. Nevertheless a general care of the buildings is not evident beyond stone masonry maintenance.

For major churches in the Catholic world, there is little to either attract a tourist or to tell the story of Catholics in the region. Indeed there is little to be found about programmes, the life of Jesus, becoming a Catholic, or encouragement for younger French people to engage with the faith.

An obvious example of this failure to communicate surrounds Richard the Lionheart, King of England and Duke of Normandy (1157-1199). Richard Coeur de Lion was a significant Christian leader during the third crusade and noted for significant victories against his Muslim counterpart Saladin (1137-1193). Whatever you make privately of this period of history, he remains one of the great medieval figures, but his tomb is not maintained with any sufficient prominence or dignity. Indeed on my visit to the cathedral, Richard's tomb was difficult to find, under its cover of gardening equipment, rakes and brooms! No candelabra, prayer desks or visitor information existed. Richard's tomb suggested an attitude of indifference to the past, at a stage in our history when Christian culture and history need to be re-highlighted. Cathedrals throughout most of their history have taught the Christian story through art, paintings, tombs and the honouring of a large, complex, yet proud history. Here Rouen Cathedral has failed in its most basic duty to imbue succeeding generations with a love and pride in our own history and culture. If the tomb of an individual such as Richard the Lionheart is worth so little and so forgotten, then how can today's younger generations be expected to understand or appreciate the thoughts, politics or religious devotion of a man such as Richard.

Catholicism makes a significant claim, that it is relevant and central to all people at all stages in world history. In our paschal candles we affirm Christ as the beginning and the end, the Alpha and the Omega, Christ as Lord of all history, yet if we allow such great medieval figures to fall into indifferent anonymity, how can we possibly argue that modern day saints such as John Paul II, John XXIII or Mary MacKillop are individuals of lasting significance?

I attended a number of Masses during my stay in Rouen, all of them celebrated with great reverence and devotion and often accompanied with beautiful cathedral music. Yet Mass attendance usually failed to reach three figures. Plainly it is not enough to have beautiful liturgy and music existing in a magnificent cathedral without any method of communicating the intentions and hopes of the Catholics within Rouen. A magnificent culture is one thing, proudly displaying and offering this to an indifferent world is another.

In all of the central churches of Rouen, tour guides were absent, and information about the cathedrals was usually missing (even in French) while there were no pictures, brochures, newspapers, advertisements about a living community to be found. No priests were available to talk to, no signage existed outside, no opportunities for making devotions were offered. The cathedrals moved somewhat into life during services, but quickly returned to dormancy at their conclusion. The overwhelming message to modern day France and those hungry for culture, history and beauty is that it's far too hard to enliven the riches of the past to ensure that it has something to offer the future. The churches of Rouen have much to be proud of in their beauty, their music and their past culture. The challenge is to enliven these so that they stimulate and inform today's Catholics and wider society.

There is much in modern Australia to be learnt from this. While we do not have cathedrals as magnificent as Rouen's, we do have a beautiful and significant history, monuments and culture of our own. And so the same question arises: Do we use our past to positively and proudly inform the present? In a society that is spending a great deal of time and effort on ancestry, the studying of the past indigenous culture, and the richness of the Anzac tradition, an obvious question arises: Where are the equivalent movements within the Catholic community? In many places, the quiet assurances of a past faith, which overcame its set of problems and which brought forth its own heroes is not available to us. Do we still feel that churches in which candles, statues, paintings of saints and devotion areas have all been removed really have anything worthwhile to say to us?

The message of Rouen is that culture, history and faith must be celebrated each day. Without this determination we subconsciously teach our children that we do not value the past nor indeed our future!

Richard the Lionheart, William the Conqueror, or the faith of the Normans were not perfect. Nevertheless, their faith generated an extremely vibrant Catholic culture which spread throughout England, Northern France, Scotland, Wales, Southern Italy, Sicily and the Middle East. It established highly individualised architecture, visual art, music and devotions. There is much to celebrate and enliven, and it deserves more than our passivity. Yet, do we say the same thing in our Australian environment?

Leipzig, Germany: a Cautionary Tale

Leipzig is a major city in the federal state of Saxony, Germany. It has been a trading city since its first documentation in 1015. The Leipzig Trade Fair was first mentioned in 1165 and continues to be of world significance even today.

In the 1500s Leipzig became a predominantly protestant city and three great battles of the Thirty Years War were fought near Leipzig. From the 16th century until World War II Leipzig was one of the leading cultural centres of Europe, particularly noted for its musicians and philosophers including Bach, Gottsched, Gillert, Schiller, Mendelssohn, Schumann and Wagner.

A vibrant Catholicism in Leipzig dates back to the 11th century and a strong Augustinian monastic foundation was also present, but from the mid-1500s following the Reformation, convents were suppressed and Catholic worship abolished. After the establishment of protestantism, Catholicism was virtually extinguished although during the 17th century small groups of Catholics were able to celebrate Mass publically. At the present time Leipzig, a city of around 500,000 people, has three Catholic parishes, two chapels and three small schools.

The two main churches in Leipzig, St Nicholas and St Thomas both have Catholic foundations but were forcibly removed from Catholic control during the Reformation.

From a Catholic cultural perspective, both of these churches are a great disappointment. It is easy to still recognise the Catholic grand design within their interiors, yet the removal of statues, most artwork, pictures, devotion to Our Lady, stations of the cross, confessionals and other devotional areas have given the church a barren and soulless feeling. Lutheran liturgical celebrations are hard to distinguish from concerts and the lack of a spiritual character sees tourists and photographers happily walking and talking throughout services.

The true nature of protestant minimalism is strongly on display with the concurrent lack of devotion to spiritual foundations. Both St Nicholas and St Thomas churches look indistinguishable from an assembly hall or concert venue and indeed it seems their main function for Leipzigers is to showcase musical events.

The 1989 communist collapse saw regular peace prayers conducted in the St Nicholas Lutheran Church, known as "Nicolai", which had become a centralised focus for peaceful resistance to the Honecker Regime. While the fall of East German communism is readily identified with the spirit of "Glasnost" and "Peristroika", coupled with the pressures of outside forces, most notably Pope John Paul II,

Margaret Thatcher and the Solidarity movement, the Nicolai Church did play an important local part in galvanising opposition to the DGR (German Democratic Republic).

Nevertheless, this peaceful intervention following the fall of communism and German reunification has not led to an increase in Christian vocations. Given German protestantism's missing cultural and spiritual underpinnings and traditional grounding any new vocations are unlikely to be brought to fruition.

St Thomas Church (Thomaskirche) is heavily connected to the life and death of composer Johann Sebastian Bach who was choirmaster from 1723-1750, taught at the nearby St Thomas free boarding school and is buried within the church. While Bach is rightly regarded as one of history's great composers, the current church has subjugated its wider role of mission and evangelism to a secular role which highlights the veneration of Bach.

It is notable that both churches suffer from lack of funds, yet a wider inability to define a Christian purpose in relation to mission to Leipzig sees these churches functioning primarily as museums.

Minimalism of liturgy, devotion and Catholic culture have removed the necessary bases for addressing a secular age. Both these churches seek to be relevant to secular Leipzig, but both continue to stand largely empty.

While in recent years Leipzig has improved its standard of living and made significant efforts to imbed itself into the global economic system, the destructive marks of communism are visibly present on almost every corner. Since reunification automobile manufacturing through BMW and Porsche has seen a "made in Germany" philosophy help Leipzig, with a substantially lower wage system than exists in West Germany. Porsche has been present in Leipzig since 1999, yet city unemployment remains above a troublesome 10 per cent.

The reality for Leipzig is that the city remains in transition with some strong pockets of revival, yet much of the city continues to slowly deteriorate in communist style buildings and infrastructure. Massive bailouts from central government will need to continue for many years as generational poverty and low wages mean many will be unable to share in this increasing prosperity.

Ironically, this is the environment in which the Catholic Church traditionally thrives, and its absence from Leipzig only highlights the "communist style" irrelevance of Leipzig's protestant churches in dealing with the economic, social and spiritual transitions into the 21st century. The Catholic social doctrine of subsidiarity has important implications in an emerging city such as Leipzig. Subsidiarity is the principle that governments should not intervene in matters that can be taken care of or resolved by families or communities. This presents a substantial challenge for Leipzig where Christian communities have failed to develop in the vacuum created by the communist demise. Without these real communities of church the faith risks becoming "individualised", without a commitment to the "body of Christ". The protestant experience has generally proven fragile at creating and sustaining such faith communities. In fact most Protestant communities are noted for fracturing along personality lines and are very susceptible to cult or sect like movements behind strong leaders.

In a vacuum between the fall of communism and the establishment of "Hypezig", the creation of real communities founded on the dignity of the human being (created in the image and likeness of God) and centred on the mystical body of Christ (in which each member contributes to the good of the whole) is yet to evolve in Leipzig.

Without a strengthening of the Catholic community in Leipzig it is hard to imagine a proper transition from destructive communism to communities that inspire both a healthy capitalism and service to the less fortunate.

Dubai, UAE: Strength in Adversity

Dubai is one of the seven emirates that make up the UAE Federation and contains within it the largest city, also called Dubai, with a population of around two million.

While the earliest historical records for Dubai date from 1095, it is really only since the 1970s that Dubai has achieved significant growth generated from oil revenues and trade.

This increased wealth has attracted a large Catholic community, mostly of Filipino, Indian or South American background. Currently this Catholic community constitutes around seven percent of the total population. Almost all of these Catholics are involved in the service industries and are at the poorer end of the Dubai community. While Catholics are free to worship, attempts to spread the faith to Muslims are prohibited. Christian men are not allowed to marry Muslim women and conversion to Christianity is forbidden. The production of Catholic material is allowed but can be problematic if not contained within the community itself.

St Mary's Dubai (established in 1989) is a church without obvious identification marks. It has no cross, no bell tower, no signage, yet it hosts a vibrant expatriate community in which around fifteen Masses are offered in English on weekends with four daily Masses on weekdays. Additionally, there are weekly and monthly Masses in other languages. This significant liturgical offering reflects the vigour and activity that is generated within the parish. A full range of confessions, baptisms, catechisms, rosary, and marriage preparation is in full swing. The parish is currently serviced by eight Capuchin priests. The church can seat around 1,700, and rarely attracts fewer than 1,500 to each weekend Mass.

The strength of this community is obvious, with ample food for thought for the Church in Australia. Undoubtedly, the relationship to the surrounding culture and community has something important to teach us. This community thrives within an Islamic context, with a culture generally indifferent to Christianity. This is not so markedly different from our own host Australian community's secular values.

In both cases, the churches are extraneous to the public sphere and in the UAE case, despite significant restrictions being placed on the ability of a Christian community to influence or engage the host society, this community continues to thrive.

The Dubai community does one thing very effectively that many Australian parishes do not. It highlights, emphasises and glorifies in Catholic culture. This is seen mostly notably in devotion to Our Lady and to the saints, particularly the newer saints who have relevance to the community, i.e., strength in adversity through examples of overcoming odds stacked against Christian life.

Devotion to Our Lady is communally strong and acts of personal piety are conspicuous and unembarrassed. The unity that the community gains from this fondness for Our Lady points to the commitment that she herself showed to her son. Within the Australian context we don't often see Our Lady as a focus of unity to energise our corporate life together. While we talk about community, we appear to have de-emphasised one of the key building blocks of community formation and sustenance.

The Dubai Catholic community fully integrates children into the spirituality of Our Lady. In this sense, they provide their children with a vehicle to resist the surrounding culture and to renew their own faith in Our Lord. Regrettably, many young Australian Catholics, even those in our schools, do not see or understand the unifying place of Mary as a guarantor of constancy and faithfulness to Jesus.

Naturally, the society in which Dubai Catholics find themselves leaves no doubt about their outsider status. Yet, concurrent with this reality, they are not seeking to belong to an Islamic worldview or philosophy. In Dubai Catholicism provides all that is necessary for a well lived life devoted to God. This parallel universe in which Catholicism is thriving is not sectarian in nature and does not seek to abandon the wider world. Rather, it bequeaths to local Catholics a better life environment in which to flourish and in which to confer a healthier spiritual and communal life for the benefit of all. The emphasis of Dubai Catholics is on tilling the soil, the growth aspect is the business of God. Dubai's Catholics are in no doubt that their faith, culture and outlook are the greatest gifts given to humanity and have ceased to seek anything else.

The outlook in Australian parish life is currently more opaque. Significantly, we have not identified the true nature of our Australian host philosophy: secularism. This failure to see secular ideas as inimical to Catholicism often means that individual Catholics formulate their views in a dual world, secularised and faith generated. This situation regularly results in clashes of philosophies with outcomes that usually lead to feet in both camps. Australian parishes that have removed or devalued devotion to Our Lady have disconnected the faith from a central Catholic cultural pillar. The Son of God became a man for our salvation, yet only after Mary's "yes" to the divine plan. The parochial identification of Mary also helps to unite Catholics in local areas with universal Catholic culture. Mary is a unique symbol of Catholic culture and most Australians are clearly aware of her identification with Catholicism.

Strengthening Mary will contribute to the strengthening of Australian parishes. The Catholics of Dubai have also established the centrality of the saints, at least in their enhancement of Catholic culture. This makes a great deal of sense as it highlights those who have overcome obstacles to live out their Catholic faith. It also connects our world strongly with apostolic beginnings, but more importantly it encourages those who may be dispirited to persevere and endure. The humanity of saints highlights what we are all called to be, but also encourages us to believe that this future is obtainable.

In recent times the lives of saints who have resisted systems hostile to Catholicism have provided excellent models. Rupert Meyer, Bernard Lichtenberg, Max Kolbe and Edith Stein are just some of those who resisted the Nazis, but their aversion was in play long before atrocities against minorities and attacks on the Church commenced. A primary strength of the saints has been to alert us to those philosophies and cultures inimical to Catholicism long before any overt persecution evolves. It is not without divine inspiration that Charles de Foucauld is still an example to Christians throughout North Africa. The Church in Australian needs a greater identification with our own Catholic exemplars who can point out the true realities of current Australian life.

In 1932 Edith Stein wrote to Pope Pius XI to highlight to him her understanding of the Nazi Challenge to Catholicism,

> As a child of the Jewish people, who by the grace of God has also been for the past 11 years a child of the Catholic Church, I dare to speak to the father of Christianity about that which oppresses millions of Germans. For weeks we have seen deeds perpetrated in Germany which mock any sense of justice and humanity, not to mention love of neighbour. For years the leaders of National Socialism have been preaching hatred of the Jews ... but the responsibility must fall, after all, on those who brought them to this point and it also falls on those who keep silent in the face of such happenings (Edith Stein, Letter to Pope Pius XI).

Here is a powerful example of what saints can offer our Catholic community. We weaken our Australian Catholicism when we ignore their voice.

Sheik Mohammad of Dubai has determined that he will not allow a competition of ideas in the UAE. Additionally, he has determined that he will not allow Christian displays or symbols that may encourage an environment of religious freedom.

Like all who seek to limit the spread of ideas, fear is never far away. Given a place within Dubai's public sphere, I have no doubt that Catholicism would soon influence the society in good ways, as yet unseen.

Nevertheless, the approach of Dubai's Catholic community is the correct one. The emphasis on culture, Our Lady and the saints of the Church has given this community a vital and coherent identity which is not only sustaining itself (without the gift of real freedom) but has transcended the barriers placed upon it.

Dresden: New growth from humble resilience

Dresden is the capital city of the Free State of Saxony in Germany. Historically, Dresden was the principal residence for the kings and electors of Saxony and has been a cultural, educational and political centre since the 12th century. Dresden's history in the modern era has been controversial, particularly during World War II when British and American bombing raids destroyed all of the inner city during the night raids of 13-15 February 1945. The anniversary of the event draws thousands of demonstrators who have used the event for various political purposes: an anti-Western event during the communist years, a peace rally post-reunification and in recent years a forum for neo Nazi rejuvenation.

Catholics have also suffered greatly in Dresden's historical narrative. The Diocese of Meissen was established in 968 to undertake the conversion of the original Slavic settlers. In the 11th century German colonisers entered the area and the first church "of Our Lady" was established in 1080.

Franciscans and Augustinians also established monastic houses over the next three centuries.

The expression of the protestant Reformation in Dresden was particularly harsh. Catholicism was proscribed and Catholics were forbidden to settle in the area.

In 1649 the Saxon Elector, Augustus the Strong, converted to Catholicism in order to claim the Polish crown, yet the condition of Catholics improved only marginally despite the construction of a Catholic cathedral in 1726. In 1806 Catholics were finally granted almost equal rights under Saxon law, while the foundation of churches and monasteries remained forbidden by the 1831 constitution.

The Catholic Cathedral (Kathedrale Sanctissimae Trinitatis) is strongly connected to the Saxon Royal family, yet this has not historically resulted in conversion to Catholicism. Saxon's Catholics number around 140,000 or three per cent of the population.

At the beginning of the 21st century Catholicism in Saxony is under immense pressure. Across Germany, clergy abuse scandals have seen a decline of 6.8 per cent in Catholic numbers over a 12 month period.

In 2010 there were only 1,100 baptisms for the whole diocese of Dresden-Meissen with only 33 adults seeking membership. In contrast, 1,078 renounced their attachment to the diocese.

In some ways Dresden is in a similar position to Leipzig with a traditionally non-Catholic population, the experience of 45 years of communism, and a lack of clergy and ministry resources.

Nevertheless, Dresden has some natural advantages. The Kathedrale Sanctissimae Trinitatis is at last in the process of restoration post-1945 and beginning to function as a cathedral should, although its interior still displays protestant austerity. The community that regularly worships there is comparatively young and has sought to attract the many visitors to the Cathedral into a deeper understanding of the Catholic faith.

Interesting talks, a bookstore, after Mass gatherings and the possibility of talking to a priest are more readily available than in Leipzig. The intention of engaging with the secular world and wider community is in greater evidence.

Additionally, while Dresden has suffered greatly from protestant and communist hostility, the current theological and cultural vacuum presents the Catholic Church with profound possibilities. Since there is no other philosophy or lifestyle option that engages with the local community, the Church has a number of opportunities to engender faith to a wider community that generally has no underlying philosophy of life. The population is unquestionably looking for change. Dresden is one of the fastest growing cities in Germany, and amongst the former East German cities has actually gained in population with its average age of 43 the lowest in Saxony.

Unmistakably Dresden is seeking to regain an earlier cultural and artistic heritage. Naturally this correlates strongly with the beauty of Catholic life, architecture, music and liturgy.

In this spirit, Dresden could engage more persuasively with artistic entities, both locally and worldwide. The Cathedral in particular could consider an annual festival showcasing world Catholic culture to a population underwhelmed by religious puritanism. Celebrations that feature music, food and entertainment, perhaps featured on a saint's day, have the potential to strengthen the Catholic community and evangelise at the same time. In a growing and youthful population, Catholic schools, education and the transmission of the faith are central. Ways must be found to increase contact with young families particularly around schools and sporting activities. The invitation to faith discovery must be free and easily accessible for all interested adults and families. Opportunities in every suburb, town hall and library should be considered to highlight the Catholic faith and contrast this with the barrenness of secular life.

St Paul has proposed a view of Christian life that is central to Dresden's future: "Christ set us free so that we should remain free. Stand firm, then, and do not let yourselves to be fastened again to the yoke of slavery" (Galatians 5:1). Dresden's Catholics must be bold in recognising the significant opportunities that exist in the east of Germany. The Church has survived the minimalism of protestantism and the tyranny of communism. Now is an opportunity for a significant Catholic development of small communities and local power. Dresden has a key opportunity in the public space to affirm the importance of Western civilisation and the key role the Catholic Church has always held within it.

Catholicism's great appeal, reaffirmed by Pope Francis, is always of a society that challenges government paternalism and lives within structures that do not show contempt for people.

The Catholic doctrine of subsidiarity is an organising principle in which local matters ought to be handled by the least centralised authorities. The principle presupposes that the autonomy and dignity of human needs are best supported, developed and sustained at the local level.

As this Catholic form of society has had no recent history in Germany, being radically different from protestantism, Nazism and communism it offers a new model to a society long ravaged by corrupt big governments where individuality was subordinated to the state.

The British philosopher Roger Scruton has made some important points in relation to post-communist societies and their emergence over the last thirty years.

Scruton rightly highlighted the role of Catholicism as "consecrating that which is not to be traded". Human equality, family life, faith and culture cannot be reduced to a market value without the risk of their destruction.

For Scruton, economics alone is not the basis for a social order. A fundamental claim of the Catholic Church is that social order can only be stabilised, enhanced and upheld by the benefit of Catholic faith which is intrinsic and irreplaceable within it.

Within the Dresden context protestantism, communism and the current post-Christian society have failed to protect the cultural and religious aspects of the community. Plainly there is a disconnection between the Catholic statement of these values and its local acceptance. In a diocese faced with losing Catholics at an annual rate of 6 per cent a coherent vision may not be adequately articulated.

Nevertheless, Catholicism must consign its own difficulties to a secondary level. The clergy abuse scandal has eroded confidence in the Church in Germany, yet now is not the time to withdraw from its historic mission and call. In a vulnerable, rootless society no longer able to recognise or affirm cultural or spiritual values, the Church in Dresden must step into this vacuum.

The formation of a community life, which is both aesthetic and spiritual (Christ-centred) is a most radical idea within German society. Additionally, a community that fosters a loyalty to these values strengthens both the family and individuals in a world that increasingly values self-determination and wealth above all else. Dresden Catholicism is faced with a society radically detached from itself. Catholic beauty, unity and community are the only answers that can satisfy.

Lourdes: Gentle Healing for All

Lourdes is a small market town lying in the foothills of the Pyrenees in southern France.

Until 1858 Lourdes was a modest town of some 4,000 people, but in February of that year, a local girl Bernadette Soubirous, claimed to have witnessed an apparition of "a beautiful lady" at a small grotto (Massabielle). These apparitions occurred on 18 occasions, with the lady identifying herself as the "Immaculate Conception". The Roman Catholic Church has authenticated these apparitions as genuine revelations of the Blessed Virgin Mary.

An estimated 200 million people have visited the town since 1860, and currently around six million pilgrims per year attend. Connected to the pilgrimage is the drinking of or bathing in Lourdes water which flows from the Grotto. While the water has no unusual properties, the Church has officially recognised some 69 miraculous healings, with hundreds of thousands additionally claiming unverified curative results. The town's current permanent population is around 40,000.

The Grotto, Crypt, Basilica and other churches are all classic in building style, well maintained, but through their designs offer an unambiguous experience of beauty and mystery.

Underlying the experience of Lourdes is the spirituality of Bernadette and her experience of Our Lady. This spirituality of humanity, gentleness and confident acceptance of divine plans contrasts strongly with the temporal values of our modern world. This distinctive approach does resonate in a feminine milieu in which quiet determination, persistence and lack of display are apparent. I was fortunate to visit in January 2014 when crowds were at a minimum. Nevertheless, the spirituality of Our Lady of Lourdes can be found strongly in all those associated with the Shrine: those offering care, guidance and support, as well as those working in more mundane roles.

In Bernadette and Our Lady, a powerful resonance, with ordinariness, compassion and a care for the forgotten and those who suffer is manifest. Lourdes is built on the small, yet abiding contribution of pilgrims who have undergone hardship and privation in their lives without yielding to despair. All through Lourdes, in the Grotto, in shrines and in the churches, small messages of hope, thankfulness and encouragement prevail.

Those who have seen something of God's compassion in their lives have sought to give this to others, particularly those without hope.

The shrines at Lourdes are beautiful, but their real beauty is found in the message that little things matter and that God is found most often in humility, service, persistence and abiding hope.

Catholic culture and identity are evident from the willingness of so many people who are affected with this desire to not share their pain and suffering but to point to hope and a better future.

Lourdes is a powerful example of Catholic culture, revealed in the courage of simple people. The Grotto, shrines, gardens and places of devotion are all different, yet contain a fundamental simplicity.

While Crypt and Basilica are classical buildings, their ornateness is not overwhelming and space for quiet and simple devotion is everywhere. The image of Our Lady of Lourdes is also simple and understated but capable of resonating with all who visit.

The appearances of Our Lady of Lourdes also highlight an important aspect of Catholic culture and belief; the slim veneer between heaven and earth. This has been one of Catholicism's overriding insights generally not shared by other Christians, that in practical ways this life is continued into the next. A "big picture" view that what we do in this life is carried into the next is at the heart of Catholic hope.

Our Lady of Lourdes is a theological picture of continuity between her appearances in the Grotto and the natural communication between God and humanity which continues into today.

The basis of Bernadette's spirituality is that God does communicate to us and that God is vitally interested in our well-being. This is a major expression of Catholicism's core belief that God intervenes in the life of humans and that his salvific activity is manifested through allowing oneself to become a vehicle for Christ's redeeming activity.

Lourdes expresses in great clarity that God cares, that miracles are part of the diving plan and that the smallest and most inconsequential people are central to the plans fulfilment. Lourdes is in my mind a clear extension of the humility of Mary, who allows herself to be a partner in God's purpose and who reveals a Jesus whose central focus is to carry the burdens of others.

Lourdes outlines another aspect of Catholicism that is often forgotten or thought not to be important: sometimes those in the church are not always at their best. The spirituality of Lourdes is not about being at our best, but about a faith that delivers the goods. The action of individuals (often imperfect) in offering prayer, forgiveness and practical healing to both individuals and to our society is a clear statement that for God's purposes: Catholicism works! At Lourdes, this practical reality is placed before the world, peace, joy and reassurance is worked through this particular Catholic place for the benefit of millions. Lourdes contains an extraordinary example of practiced Catholic culture that actually works for others.

In Our Lady of Lourdes, a positive vision of the future is already seen as a present reality, and the true meaning of our life's experience through vibrant Catholicism is there for all to see.

4

CATHOLICITY AND WESTERN CULTURE

Catholic Centrality to Western Civilisation

The Neolithic Revolution, which witnessed the widespread transition of hunter-gatherer small groups of humans to one of agricultural development and permanent settlement, undoubtedly marks the advent of civilisation.

These changes in the human condition necessitated new structures in organisation and rapidly witnessed the development of formalised religion, the initial experience of commerce and the usage of particularised writing systems.

Accompanying these material changes was the entrance of a radically different type of human being, one who could operate with a much wider division of labour, whose concept of group affiliation was larger and who saw the usefulness of relations with others for trade and defence as requisite.

The striking feature of these initial civilisations, continued into modern times, has been one of expansion, developing prosperity followed by decline and eventual ruin.

Nevertheless, there is one civilisation that so far seems to be an exceptional case, not conforming to these vagaries of expansion, prosperity and permanent decline. That civilisation is commonly designated as Western civilisation.

Western civilisation seems to contain two distinct aptitudes, not found in other civilisations. Firstly, a profound receptivity to new ideas and a spirit of innovation, particularly in relation to design and production; and secondly, the theological virtue and praxis of the Catholic Church.

The role of the city is essential in Western civilisation. The cultural and trade centres of Athens, Rome, London, Paris and New York, along with a host of others, have seen cultural, artistic and industrial excellence develop, where close personal interaction and competition exist.

In a similar way, the early centres of Christianity were the major trading core of the ancient world. Antioch, Alexandria, Athens, Rome and Constantinople were particularly attractive to early Christians, as many of these first followers of Jesus were merchants.

By the second century, Christianity had spread east into Persia and central Asia, again along trading lines, continuing the tradition of itinerant missionaries who often doubled as merchants and tradesmen.

Following the reign of the Emperor Constantine (272-337) Catholicism developed a decisive relationship with imperial politics. However, from the very beginning the Bishop of Rome has always claimed a biblical mandate (Matthew 16:18) for this leadership role throughout the wider Church. Noticeably, from its earliest emergence, Catholicism has played a central role in education and the development of philosophy, ideas and doctrine that would act in integrating and unifying Western civilisation. Catholicism continues to fulfil this mandate into current times.

The political philosopher Philippe Nemo from the Ecole Superieure de Commerce de Paris (European Business School of Paris) in his book *What is the West* has identified two wings of Western civilisation. For Nemo differences can be identified between an Anglo-Saxon derivative and a continental European variant. Nevertheless,

Nemo stresses that such differences as do exist are not central to the common heritage that distinguishes them.

Nemo pinpoints a number of steps in the unfolding of Western civilisation. These structures have continued as an essential bedrock for Western thought, while also transitioning into new and vibrant forms which continue to provide cultural and scientific expansion.

At base is a combination of cultural, scientific and theological partnerships that have remained essential to Western civilisation from its beginnings to its current expression.

Philosophy

The Greek establishment of the city state (*polis*) inaugurated a society in which theoretically all citizens were expected to participate in the political and administrative life of the community.

The Australian Professor of Economics, Wolfgang Kasper, in *The Merits of Western Civilisation* rightly concludes that this new form of society ensured that citizens were no longer subjected to the arbitrary whims of rulers but were bound to sets of rules and principles established at public gatherings.

Rational argument distinguished Greek law and politics and implied not only that community life could be improved by rationality but also that the natural and religious world could be subject to such inquiry. Almost 28 centuries later Pope John Paul II in his encyclical *Faith and Reason* (*Fides et Ratio*) commented in the prologue to the document:

> Faith and reason are like two wings on which the human spirit arises to the contemplation of truth; and God has placed in the human heart a desire to know the truth – in a word, to know himself – so that by knowing and loving God, men and women may also come to the fullness of truth about themselves (*Fides et Ratio*, Prologue).

This initiative of Greek civilisation has always been at the heart of Catholicism and still today the Church takes seriously this foundational relationship:

> Sure of her competence as the bearer of the Revelation of Jesus Christ, the Church reaffirms the need to reflect upon truth. This is why I have decided to address you, my venerable Brother Bishops, with whom I share the mission of "proclaiming the truth openly" (2 Corinthians 4.2) as also theologians and philosophers whose duty it is to explore the different aspects of truth, and all those who are searching; and I do so in order to offer some reflections on the path which leads to true wisdom, so that those who love truth, may take the sure path leading to it and so find rest from their labours and joy for their spirit" (*Fides et Ratio*, 6).

Catholicism clearly claims a divine mandate in the Revelation of Jesus Christ, to both build on understanding the rationality of the Greek philosophers and to expand and uphold the rational shaping of Western social ideas and praxis.

Law

Nemo demonstrates another foundational tenet of Western thought, generated within the ancient Roman Republic. Roman Law embraces the legal developments of over 1,000 years from the beginnings of the Republic in 450 BC through to the Justinian Code (Corpus Juris Civito) in 529 AD.

This *Jus Civile* or Citizen's Law, was the body of Common Law that applied to Roman citizens. This Law, coupled with the Roman Constitution (*mos maiorum*) which was passed down mainly by precedent, developed concepts that continue to live on in our modern practice of law. The separation of powers, vetoes, quorum requirements, term limits, impeachments and checks and balances are all aspects of Roman Law that remain today.

These Roman Laws were also founded on the beginnings of a deeper concept of natural law, which implied a concept of "human nature" and a set of inalienable rights associated with all humans. Natural law also has a strong reliance on the use of reason to deduce binding rules of moral behaviour.

Once more, it has been the Catholic Church which has upheld the application of natural law vigorously throughout history and its current moral and ethical applications. The Catholic view of natural law holds that human beings consist of body and mind, the physical and non-physical (soul) and that they are capable through the use of reason and conscience to determine actions and thoughts as good or evil.

The Catholic position has been exhibited most clearly in the work of St Thomas Aquinas (1225-1274):

> There belongs to the natural law, first, certain most general precepts, that are known to all; and second, certain secondary and more detailed precepts, which are, as it were, conclusions following closely from first principles (*Summa Theologica* (1-11 Q 99A6).

For Catholics, natural law is concerned with both action and motive and not simply a case of right actions but of right motive as well. This understanding remains at the forefront of Western morality of which the major voice continues to be the Catholic Church.

Western civilisation is impossible without the ancient Roman clarification of the individual persona and his various freedoms, yet still more important is the Catholic revelation that Jesus Christ is the visible image of God.

> God, having in the past spoken to the fathers through the prophets at many times and in various ways, has at the end of these days spoken to us by his son, whom he appointed heir of all things, through whom also he made the world.

His son is the radiance of his glory, the very image of his substance (Hebrews 1:3).

This Catholic view of *Imago Dei* has contributed overwhelmingly to the concept of modern "human rights". The belief that all humans are fundamentally equal in rights and freedoms has influenced documents such as the United States Declaration of Independence and the Universal Declaration of Human Rights; yet at their heart remains an intrinsically Catholic conviction.

Judeo-Christian theology has influenced conceptions of human rights in another more profound way. Catholics do not have a theological, philosophical or moral perspective that emphasises nihilism or post-modernism. The core of Western civilisation constantly emphasised by Catholics is that humanity can be improved and nourished through the proper use of reason and scientific, democratic and Catholic values.

This non-fatalistic Catholic world-view continues to encourage scientific, political and moral improvements. Social welfare, compassion and concern for others remain at the heart of Western civilisation and are constantly critiqued and encouraged by the Catholic Church, particularly with renewed vigour under the current papacy of Pope Francis.

While many proponents of Western civilisation would agree with the inclusion of Greek and Roman influences in the formation of its fundamental essence, others would concentrate more exclusively on impacts from the Renaissance and the French Revolution, highlighting a stream of Western culture which came to fruition around 1400 AD.

In my view this is a Spartan understanding of Western civilisation. The Renaissance, primarily a cultural movement and the French Revolution with its political impact, still stand within the greater narrative of Western civilisation. The Renaissance thinkers did not reject Catholicism, in fact, most of its art and culture were devoted to Catholicism and largely supported by the Church. The French Revolution certainly caused a massive shift in power from Church to State, encouraged great resentment against Catholics and during the reign of terror included the murder of priests and destruction of churches. Nevertheless, the 1801 concordat between Napoleon and Pope Pius VII ended this anti-Catholic period solidified the Catholic Church as the majority church of France and restored its civil status.

The comprehensive and expansive nature of Catholic impact upon Western civilisation can be shown in the writings and actions of Christian thinkers, popes, monastic life, architecture, education, mission and saints. The closeness of this relationship can be seen from the inception of Christianity through to the current day.

Augustine of Hippo (354-430) supported Christian belief with the learning, logic and philosophy he had obtained through the study of pagan classics. Augustine considered faith to be of primary importance yet human reason was the essential means for understanding the revelation of faith. Augustine's great achievement was the establishment of the connection between Catholic faith and human reason, a legacy that continues until the present time.

Politics

In 800 AD Charles (later Charlemagne) King of the Franks was crowned Emperor, and Augustus in Rome by Pope Leo III.

Charlemagne's imperial intentions seemed founded on the re-establishment of the Roman Empire. Certainly, the use of Latin, the expansion of Catholicism, the monasteries and church officials and a favourable Pope in Rome gave Charlemagne a unique opportunity to re-constitute Rome.

Significantly, Charlemagne aspired to provide a religious and ideological coherence to his diverse empire. Both Pope Leo III and

Charlemagne recognised that uniting imperial and spiritual authority would benefit both. Bishops and abbots with administrative skills became endowed with land and working peasants which bestowed significant income and added another layer of authority to local lords. Charlemagne's empire contained over 600 monasteries, which primarily centred Carolingian loyalty to Catholicism over ethnic groupings.

Byzantium

The Byzantine expression of the Roman Empire (330-1453) maintained a close connection to the process of blending Church and State. The Emperor Justinian (527-565) adopted a policy of "one God, one empire, one religion" with the intention of imposing legal and doctrinal conformity. Justinian's legal code, the Corpus Juris Civilis (Body of Civil Law) was used in both East and West, was taught in Bologna in the 12th century and still in use at the beginning of the Renaissance. Justinian's code has been the foundation for both English common law and subsequent European law.

Justinian was also an extensive builder. During his reign noteworthy churches, monasteries and palaces arose throughout the empire. His most famous construction, the Hagia Sophia Church (Holy Wisdom), completed in 537, is still with us today and one of the masterpieces of world architecture.

In both East and West, monasticism grew in popularity, providing a method of religious perfection and communal life. Significantly, monasteries became great centres of learning as well as providing care for orphans, widows and the sick from surrounding communities. In Western monasticism, the rule of St Benedict (480-547) encouraged a disciplined balance between work and devotion. The critical organisational benefits of monastic life ensured their significant contribution to Western civilisation in the economic, political and spiritual domains up to the present day.

The Papacy

The doctrine of Papal primacy plays a key role in ensuring the integrity of Catholicism, particularly in relation to secular power or political and religious systems hostile to the Church. This doctrine based on the words of Jesus in Matthew's Gospel (16:18), "You are Peter and upon this rock I will build my Church," authorised subsequent Popes to claim leadership of the Catholic Church. Article I of the *Code of Canon Law* grants to the Roman Pontiff "supreme, full, immediate and universal power in the Church, that he can always and freely exercise".

The advent of an assertive papacy has had a major impact on Western civilisation linking law and philosophy, but more importantly encouraging ethical engagement and practical actions towards the improvement of others as normative. This is not evident in any significant measure in the philosophies of Buddhism, Hinduism, Islam, modern ideologies or new age paganisms.

This "conscience" function of the modern papacy has seen the vigorous opposition to National Socialism in the encyclical of Pope Pius XI, *Mit Brennender Sorge* (With Burning Anxiety) which was smuggled into Nazi Germany and read in all Catholic parishes on 21 March 1937. The encyclical condemns the elevation of one race above others, denounces the practice of eugenics and the false idolisation of the state.

In the 1980s Pope John Paul II was also at the forefront of the conflict with communism. Lech Walesa, the founder of the anti-communist workers movement Solidarity, recognised John Paul II as providing the necessary heroic leadership to inspire the Polish people to reject communism. Two former communist leaders, the Polish General Jaruzelski and former Soviet President, Mikhail Gorbachev, both agree that the collapse of the Soviet Union and Eastern European communism would not have been possible without the "principled stand for peace and freedom that inspired millions to topple tyranny".

Pope Benedict XVI and Pope Francis have both continued this tradition of engagement in public life. Both men have been noted for their humility, their concern for the poor and their commitment to dialogue with people of all backgrounds or faiths.

Art and Architecture

Throughout its history Catholicism has always sought to emphasise the transformation of humanity in the life of Jesus through art, architecture and objects of beautiful design. In the great churches of Rome, Byzantium and throughout the world, cathedrals, parishes, monasteries, convents and schools have endeavoured to convey the message of Christ, the dignity of the Trinity, the devotion of Our Lady and the mission of the laity, to all who encounter them.

Catholicism has initiated a number of distinctive styles of church architecture that have influenced not only fellow Catholics, but also humanity's actual process of thinking and learning.

Romanesque, Gothic and Norman styles have all developed within differing Catholic cultures and emphasised assorted aspects of the Church's revelation. These styles have often adopted local building traditions to produce a synthesis that exhibits both universal and parochial theological emphases. The role, character and symbolism of cathedrals should not be underestimated. They have throughout history not only spoken of the connection between bishop, priest and community, but also of hopes, purposes and aspirations of communities and nations. In every city where Catholic cathedrals are found events of great local and world significance have occurred, usually emphasising the human struggle for justice, equity and truth.

Religious Orders and Monastic Life

The Catholic Church also impacted on society in a number of unexpected ways. The clergy was one of the first professions to adopt a largely merit based structure. Certainly, nepotism and aristocratic appointments were made on a regular basis, but increasingly seminary training rendered family and class connections less substantive. The results of this meritocracy showed in the formation of new orders, often founded on the actions of charismatic individuals, with many concentrating on various aspects of community, including education, hospitals, prisons and a host of other initiatives.

Given the profound way the work of the orders has contributed to a Catholic culture and identity, the issues that currently face Australian Catholics are made more challenging, due to the small numbers and general lack of prominence of the orders in their traditional fields.

Additionally, the Franciscans, Jesuits and Dominicans, Benedictines and other orders have influenced the wider society through their education, charisms, and devotion to particular ideals. Importantly, the orders have offered an insightful example of how to be highly focused and specific, yet still remain part of the wider Catholic faith and culture.

Education

Education has been central to the essential identity and character of Catholicism since Apostolic times. From the advent of the 12th century cathedral schools provided formation for prospective clergy, but by the end of that century had broadened the curriculum to include students for secular vocations. From 200AD onwards, lawyers, doctors, teachers, notaries and merchants, who were not studying for the priesthood but who required quality Latin, were taught concurrently with future clergy. The earliest universities grew out of these cathedral schools. The University of Paris is a typical example of this transformation having evolved from the theological college, Sorbonne, in the mid-12th century.

South America

The discovery of the Americas (15th-16th centuries) extended the reach of Western civilisation and shifted commercial and cultural emphasis away from central Europe and the Mediterranean and to the Atlantic nations of Spain and Portugal. The resultant extensions of Western civilisation into South America did result initially in economic corruption and exploitation. Nevertheless Catholicism's lasting legacy has continued to be to educate, aid and support these South American nations until today.

Roman Catholic clergy who accompanied these explorations and trade settlements were particularly concerned not only to extend the Catholic faith but also to inculcate Western learning and civilisation. The periodic harshness of Spanish and Portuguese conduct in South America did see many priests work unceasingly not only for conversions but also for regulations and legislation to protect the Indian inhabitants from the worst examples of corruption and abuse.

The development of monastic culture in South America saw an increasing emphasis not only on teaching the faith but in teaching and expanding economic progression and security. The record of the Church in these endeavours is overwhelmingly beneficial, despite retrospective criticisms that have arisen in later years.

Protestantism

In 1517 European Catholicism faced a critical confrontation with the promulgation of Martin Luther's 95 theses, generally regarded as the beginning of the Protestant Reformation.

Luther notably focused on the selling of indulgences for the remission of sins as a violation of Catholic teaching but also challenged a number of other Catholic doctrines such as papal centrality, baptism of infants and the real presence of Christ in the Eucharist.

Catholicism then embarked on a period of self-reform (known as the Counter Reformation) during the 16th and early 17th centuries in which it abolished exploitative practices and re-orientated itself towards mission particularly in Africa, Asia and the Americas. The convoking of the Council of Trent in 1545 eradicated much of the confusion on Catholic doctrines, particularly sacramental life and the real presence in the Eucharist. Nonetheless, perhaps the most profound change happened in the self-reform of parish and community life. The Jesuits (Society of Jesus, founded 1534) were at the forefront of the movement of spiritual change. Their distinctive Ignatian spirituality emphasised both a close link with the papacy and radical ministry that avoided ecclesiastical preferment. Their strong emphasis on mission to the most far flung regions (China, Japan, South America) and their emphasis on education, schools and intellectual activity led them to implanting Christian teaching, coupled with Western ways of thinking in the New World.

A good example of this renewed energy in the Church was Francis Xavier (1506-1552) who undertook extensive missionary work into modern day China, Japan, India and Indonesia. Xavier placed great emphasis on learning the language of these missionary territories and notably tried to understand the cultural environment in which these societies were formed. Xavier consistently sought to substantiate Christian principles within aspects of local culture in ways he believed would give additional creditability to Catholicism. His focus on cultural aspects of ministry led Xavier towards the assimilation of local cultural understandings into a format that was essentially Western in nature.

Science

At the onset of the 17th century, the emergence of modern science witnessed changing perceptions about the role of the scientist, the value of evidence, experimentation and the intellectual movement towards empiricism. Despite an increasing emphasis on reason and knowledge, most notable early scientists, including Copernicus, Brahe, Kepler, Galileo, Bacon, Newton, Descartes, Pascal and Liebniz, were devout in their faith. This reality has encouraged many academics to see a direct relationship between Catholic metaphysics and the advent of the scientific revolution.

Further Reading

Chris Berg, *In Defence of Freedom of Speech*, Institute of Public Affairs, 2012.

Wolfgang Kasper, *The Merits of Western Civilisation*, Institute of Public Affairs, 2012.

5

CATHOLICISM AND THE WEST

Beyond Nationalism

Towards the end of the 18th century, nationalism developed as a dominant political phenomenon within Western civilisation. Nationalism is a belief that the individual owes political and psychological loyalty to a secular nation state. Nationalism can also imply the reverse idea where within world politics, particular nations have come to be identified with particular groups of people (i.e., Han Chinese with China). Prior to the last 300 years, the Roman Empire was the great ideal of a universal world state. Christianity and Western civilisation both sought to reside within and support this wider identity. Catholics have never lost this attachment to a wider political identification than just a nation state. In German history there have been two examples of persecution of Catholics (Kulturkampf 1873 and the Nazis 1933-45) both based on nationalist fears that Catholic Germans would owe allegiance primarily to the Church or the papacy above an emerging Germany. Both Bismarck and Hitler persecuted Catholics and were unwilling to allow bishops and priests to have any real voice in German political life.

Blessed Clement August Graf von Galen, Bishop of Munster (Germany) during World War II denounced Nazi euthanasia policies, Gestapo terror and the persecution of the German Catholic Church. While Von Galen was actually a staunch German patriot, he saw his political allegiance as resting on something much greater than Germany alone. In a similar manner, Bernard Lichtenberg was an outspoken priest in Berlin, firstly in Charlottenberg and then at St Hedwig's in Berlin. Lichtenberg would pray publically for persecuted Jews and often protested individually to Nazi officials over their organised murder of the mentally ill. Lichtenberg was arrested but died in transit to Dachau concentration camp. Both men were part of a significant Catholic resistance to National Socialism and highlighted the Catholic propensity to see beyond the national state as the arbiter of personal identity or morality.

The Church has always stressed general regard for humanity, the right to life of all, including the unborn, the mentally ill and the elderly, faith in natural law and belief in Jesus Christ as central to human history and future welfare. Nation states that neglect these marks of human life and culture will always find themselves in opposition to Catholicism.

Industry

The industrial revolution emerged almost concurrently with the scientific revolution but had as its focal point improvements in chemical and iron processes, increased efficiency in water and steam generation and the development of machine tools. For many historians the industrial revolution marks a turning point in history, where for the first time the living standards of the majority working classes began to rise. These increases in real wages, life expectancy and middle class numbers have paralleled the emergence of the modern capitalist economy. The changes experienced by ordinary people have been the most profound in human history.

Nevertheless, initial problems in this transition to a modern society included a disparity of wealth between those who owned the means of production and those who worked within it.

Socialism and Communism

Socialism sought to improve the industrial system by placing an emphasis on public ownership and control of these expanding enterprises.

While some socialists were Catholics, most were not and indeed were hostile to the teachings of the Church. Communism evolved out of socialist theories and was advocated strongly by Karl Marx (1818-1883) and Friedrich Engels (1820-1895) both of whom highlighted materialistic improvement as a central tenet of human life and dignity, coupled with a militant atheism.

Once more in papal history both Pius IX (1792-1878) and Leo XIII (1810-1903) sought to correct basic errors, in this instance, in socialism and communism. Leo XIII's encyclical *Rerum Novarum* introduced the idea of "subsidiarity", the principle that political and social decisions should be taken at the local level. Unfortunately, most socialists and communists came to regard Catholicism as a primary enemy and often sought to portray their political systems as a replacement for Catholicism.

The establishment of communism in the Soviet Union in 1917 and in China in 1949 resulted in large scale persecution of Catholics and other Christians in both countries.

In the Soviet Union, the communist state was committed to the destruction of religion, destroying churches, harassing and executing priests and flooding schools with atheistic teaching. The estimated number of Christian deaths during the Soviet period is between 12-20 million.

Ironically, with the German invasion of the Soviet Union in 1941, Joseph Stalin, the Soviet leader (1878-1953), revived the Russian Orthodox Church to increase patriotic resistance to the Germans. Stalin recognised that religious identity was a stronger unifying and resisting force than communist rhetoric.

Following the Soviet victory in 1945 the churches again endured a substantial and sustained persecution which now included many Catholics incorporated within the Warsaw Pact nations, who formed a broad extended Soviet buffer zone with Western nations.

During the socialist/communist period the Church sought to support Catholics by developing a large number of new organisations designed to cultivate and protect Catholics in different professions.

Workers, tradesmen, teachers, war veterans and labour unions all sought to devote service to the betterment of the lives of Catholics, particularly in education and fraternal associations. At the same time, many new devotional societies sprang up, particularly the Legion of Mary, as well as the Marian Shrines of Lourdes and Fatima. These new organisations coupled with the social work of the St Vincent de Paul Society and a host of new charitable organisations greatly strengthened and enhanced Catholic unity, speaking both to the Church's foundational role in Western civilisation but also in resisting the modern heresies of socialism and communism.

One particular organisation that was highly successful in the middle of last century was the German Catholic Centre Party which promoted enlightened social legislation but also drew members of the Church to a clearly Catholic party while reducing their exodus to the atheistic socialist and communist parties. In the face of the rampant secularisation that besets modern Australia, perhaps it is once more time to consider the political potential of Australian Catholicism.

Vatican II

The Second Vatican Council (Vatican II 1962-1965) sought to address relations between the Catholic Church and the modern world and while the Council's legacy remains contentious to this day, nevertheless the central role of Catholicism within Western civilisation continues to be affirmed with the central doctrine that the Catholic Church alone brings ultimate salvation to humanity remains a core teaching.

John Paul II

John Paul II (1920-2005) continued to explore the work of Vatican II and to reposition the Catholic Church within the modern world yet at the same time re-enforcing orthodox Catholic teachings.

In 1979 he laid out the blueprint of his pontificate in his encyclical *Redemptor Hominis*, particularly in relation to contemporary human issues. He concentrated heavily on developing a full understanding of the human person and also of the person of Christ as the redeemer of humanity. Of importance for our understanding of the relationship between Western civilisation and the Church was his clear teaching that "anyone, no matter how weak, wishing to understand himself thoroughly, must assimilate the whole reality of the incarnation and redemption in order to find himself". John Paul II clearly recognised the person of Christ and the Catholic Church as the foundational adhesive holding Western civilisation together.

Redemptor Hominis also condemned atheist-based communism as inherently inhuman. The Pope cited Augustine's understanding of God as the basis for a full understanding of humanity: "You have made us for yourself Lord, and our hearts are restless until they rest in you." Any civilisation that denies this fundamental human condition is flawed. In this essential outlook both John Paul II and St Augustine confront humanity's essential longing for God and his Church. This inter-connectedness is vital to the nature of Western civilisation and its fundamental grounding in the person of Jesus and the Catholic Church.

During the pontificate of John Paul II, the Church fully entered into a global perspective with Catholicism becoming more universalised with huge numbers of new Catholics particularly in Asia.

China: A Western Nation Without Christianity?

Since the late 1970s the Chinese Communist Government has embarked on a series of extensive policy changes. Under Paramount Leader Deng Xiaoping China began to open up to what has become the "global economy". In 1979 the Ministry of Justice was reopened and Deng conducted a five year rehabilitation of those imprisoned and persecuted during the Maoist years. The drive for economic advancement saw China adopt market practices, improve international relations and restore some religious freedoms. In the last thirty years, Chinese wealth, GDP, literacy rates and life expectancy have risen sharply. While the Government has allowed small expressions of dissent and actively encouraged an individualist philosophy coupled with the pursuit of wealth, huge questions remain over China's future, particularly without the centrality of the Catholic Church. The Chinese Government continues to reject the authority of the Vatican, notably in the appointment of bishops, but does recognise the Pope as a significant spiritual leader. Meanwhile Catholicism continues to grow in self-confidence with around 150,000 conversions per year.

Some Catholics, who recognise the authority of the Pope in his apostolic ministry, worship in secret and can be subject to arrest and harassment. Sino-Vatican relations have not yet been normalised but "quasi-official" delegations have been received in the Vatican during the papacies of John Paul II and Benedict XVI.

Many commentators on China have recognised the considerable economic growth in the country over the past 40 years. Nevertheless, China has also experienced severe disruption to communities along with the psychological, drug and alcohol problems found in societies where the individual has taken centre stage.

Without Catholicism, there is nothing to challenge the destruction that is wrought on the many individuals who lose perspective, abandon community and serve only their own interests.

Modern Australia

In Australia most of our social problems, including mental instability, drug addition, high divorce and alcoholism have one common factor: the individuals concerned are without community. Yet, this is what the central Christian doctrine of the Trinity, challenges. In the unique Christian understanding, God himself is a community (Father, Son and Holy Spirit) with the Church called as a community to enter into this divine life with the parish as an organisation both of service to its members and to their wider community. Without this notion of vocation, which sees life not as property but as a gift, human life results in little more than service to self-interest alone.

Many individuals in China are searching for something beyond themselves. This in itself confirms my contention that without Catholicism, Western civilisation is only capable of economic development. But as John Paul II has noted, this does not bring humans to the fullness of their humanity. Naturally, as many non-baptised Chinese people seek out the faith that brings fullness, we must also endeavour to ensure our own Australian society does not plummet any deeper into its own mire of individual self-absorption.

New Challenges

New challenges to Western civilisation have arisen at all stages of our history and remain with us today. A key ingredient of the Catholic life is to be attentive to these movements and to seek to challenge their opinions and beliefs, particularly when points of view seek to weaken or destroy central tenets of Western civilisation.

In 2010 a group of Australian Catholic bishops recommended that Catholics be discouraged from voting for the Australian Greens and their political affiliates. At the heart of this concern are the inherently anti-Catholic policies of the party. The Australian Greens wish to withdraw government funding from Catholic schools and coerce these schools into employing staff whose values, views or lifestyles are contrary to the Catholic faith. This is little more than an indirect attack on Catholicism, seeking to disconnect its moral code from the core of Western civilisation and to portray Catholics as upholding non-mainstream views.

The Greens Party also seeks to decriminalise personal drug use, promote gay marriage as a viable alternative to marriage between a man and a woman, and to compel medical practitioners to participate or be associated with the practice of abortion. The Greens Party also seeks legislation to legalise euthanasia.

These Green positions are not frivolous but challenges to the very heart of Western civilisation and a Catholic defence of these values. The sanctity of life and its expression both in a beginning of life and end of life ethics are at the core of what it means to be Catholic and Western.

Such assaults are not new, nor will they disappear in coming years. It is therefore imperative that the Church remain vigilant in its defence of our values.

In the last forty years the Australian education system has also moved to a position that significantly downplays the value of Western civilisation and Christianity, and encourages a host of courses not directly related to the students' life experience. The heavy influence of indigenous studies, which includes a teacher-led philosophical outlook in Australian primary schools and the almost total emphasis in university arts degrees of women and gender studies is of concern. This is not to suggest that these subjects are not worthy of inclusion in an Australian curriculum, however their current domination ensures that students leave educational institutions with no understanding of ancient history, no Australian history, no civics, no notion of parliament or democratic institutions, and no understanding of the causes of recent wars, the fight against communism or Australia's current foreign policies.

In my own time as a school chaplain (fifteen years in Victorian schools) Australian history began at the Vietnam War and conditioned students to consider our entry into that war and our allegiance with the United States to be pernicious and unjust to the Vietnamese people. When only such blatantly one-sided conclusions are presented it is not surprising that many students leave school with a sense of shame towards their own nation, people and culture.

The Australian political culture is also often inimical to Western cultural values and norms. Many Australians are earnest in their devotion to the disabled or those in financial hardship (single mums, children from broken families, the drug addict or alcoholics) yet this does not extend to the unborn or those who advocate for right to life issues. Unfortunately, this issue has become entangled with women's right to control over their bodies. This is not to suggest that this pro-women's perspective is untenable but the outcome of such an over-emphasis has meant a vast increase in the number of abortions, the horror of partial birth abortion and increasing abdication of men from responsibility and commitment to women and families. Our blind spot on this issue has ensured an increase in other social difficulties, particularly single parenthood and troubled adolescents. Abortion is not a female issue but a human one and requires a response to which both sexes are committed.

The Victorian Abortion Legislation of 2008 also has brought shame and dishonour for the Melbourne Anglican Archdiocese. An all-female committee representing the church recommended that abortion be decriminalised and that in cases of foetal abnormality, abortion was the "least problematic solution". Of particular discredit, was the position of the Archbishop, who absented himself and all Anglican men by saying he "felt men had said enough". Such views debase Christians of a protestant background but perhaps affirm again that only Catholicism is sufficiently equipped to defend the values and integrity of Western traditions and civilisation.

A number of critical considerations need to be implemented to rejuvenate the link between Catholicism and Western civilisation. Initially, we must reclaim Western culture in our schools as an understanding of ourselves, that has delivered wonderful benefits to men and women in our society, but also as a system that remains the primary beacon throughout the world against injustice, inequality and persecution. This means that institutions like the Catholic Church need to do more within their own school system to ensure that core aspects of Western civilisation are understood and valued by students who attend these schools. The cultural and philosophical background has been left vacant in most Australian schools while unfortunately the Catholic system has done no better in ensuring their students are familiar with the foundations of our culture and Western civilisation as a whole. This will require an intense long-term commitment to such studies.

At the university level, even the Australian Catholic University's Bachelor of Arts course is cluttered with strands of study such as digital journalism, health development, leisure studies, media, sociology and psychology which, while touching on aspects of Western civilisation, offer no coherent study of our past, current developments or the central nature of Catholicism within it. Courses in Contemporary World History, Transitional History, Women's and Social History, again fail to engender the necessary focus on Western civilisation or encourage deep and meaningful understandings of these central tenets of our life and culture.

The lack of attention given to classical studies, Graeco-Roman history and philosophy, our democratic ideals, our Catholic influence, and our enlightenment and scientific underpinnings, can only suggest that modern arts degrees are substantially failing in their duty to prepare students to live fully within and to appreciate Western civilisation and culture.

Further Reading

Paul Collins, *The Birth of the West: Rome, Germany, France and the Creation of Europe in the Tenth Century*, Public Affairs, New York, 2014.

Norbert Elias, *The Germans*, Columbia University Press, New York, 1998.

Anthony Grafton et el, *The Classical Tradition*, Harvard University Press, 2010.

Charles Moore, *Margaret Thatcher: From Grantham to the Falklands*, Alfred Knopf, 2013.

6

THE STRUGGLE FOR JESUS

Islam and the Uniqueness of Jesus

Islam in Australia remains a minority religion despite a substantial increase during the last 25 years. Australian census data from 1981 shows a population of 109,423 or 0.7% of the total population. By 2011 this had grown to 479,300 or 2.25%, a not insignificant increase of 438% in thirty years.

While Islam in Australia is still a tiny minority, following the 2001 New York World Trade Centre attacks, the London, Madrid and Bali bombings (88 Australian lives lost), Australians have become significantly aware of differing expressions of Islam throughout the world. Aspects of Islamic terrorism, the poor state of human rights and liberty in most Islamic states, the lack of freedom for women and the blatant persecution endured by Christians in lands where Islamic majorities exist are of major concern.

Within the Australian context in recent years, Islam has often become the most striking example of the failure of multiculturalism. Full burkas in Melbourne and Sydney streets, under age marriage difficulties, and the establishment of home grown terror cells have led many Australians to conclude that some Muslims are involved in culture wars which seek to obscure the majority Western Christian worldview.

Questions of any Islamic political dimensions in Australia are not my immediate consideration, except to note that Catholics in Australia are acutely ill-informed of the direct theological challenge from Islam at the very heart of Catholicism and formed around questions of fundamental nature, mission and integrity to the apostolic teachings of Christ.

Catholic confusion over Islam can be noticed at the highest levels. In December 2000 Pope John Paul II issued a pontifical encyclical at the end of Ramadan in which he sought to highlight the "Abrahamic" connection between Christianity, Islam and Judaism.

Within this encyclical John Paul II spoke of the common humanity in all people, both in its diversity and in its aspirations. In March 2001 John Paul II again spoke of "neighbourly relations over the centuries between Christianity and Islam" while on an official visit to Syria.

Nevertheless, even during John Paul II's pontificate, many Catholic bishops expressed an aversion to Islam's growing presence in Europe.

Archbishop Bernadini (Izmar Archdiocese Turkey) at the 1999 Bishops Synod spoke of an Islamic program of "expansion and reconquest" through immigration and petrodollars. He compared Muslim-Christian dialogue to a dialogue of the deaf. Indeed Bernadini went further and suggested that terms such as "dialogue, justice, human rights and democracy have a completely different meaning for the Muslim than for us". In October 1999, the *National Catholic Reporter* noted Catholic aversion to the use of the term "Abrahamic faiths" as it connoted an equality across the faiths that Catholic revelation cannot support. A number of scholars concurrently warned the Church of the need for firmer stances in inter-faith contexts and the necessity to resist Islamic conversions.

In 2004 Cardinal Joseph Ratzinger, later Pope Benedict XVI, expressed appreciation for Muslims, in the nature of their piety, devotion to prayer and marriage fidelity. The direction of this praise was firmly aimed at a European Western audience and amounted to a call to the West for a rediscovery of their religious values.

On other occasions Benedict has been noted as an opponent of Turkish integration into the European Union, on the grounds that an Islamic nation should not join a predominantly Christian union but properly belonged to an association of Islamic states.

This dualistic tolerance has mostly seen its expression at the peak of the Catholic hierarchy, nevertheless, the German headscarf ban brought the issue into a more grass roots level.

In 2006, eight of Germany's sixteen states banned the wearing of religious clothing or from making an ideological gesture in an effort to maintain neutrality and peace in German schools.

Initially, Christianity was exempt from the ban, but recently the Berlin City-State has banned all religious symbols in public institutions including the Christian crucifix and Jewish Kippah.

In recent years, restrictions on Islamic dress and culture have arisen in many European nations, usually on grounds of seeking to limit "marks of separation" within cultural groups.

Undeniably, ambivalence, concern and sometimes anxiety can be found towards Islam within the worldwide Catholic Church and amongst those Western communities that have experienced substantial Islamic migration in the last 30-40 years.

Recently, it has been noted that a lack of theological sophistication amongst Catholics has left many graduates of Catholic schools unable to apply their faith in either secular or religious debates. The abandoning of the faith beyond the school years and the lack of any ongoing meaningful expression of Catholicism is of considerable concern to the Church as these serve to undermine the wonder of Catholic revelation and the accomplishment of its mission.

The most recent challenge to the Church in Australian comes from the Islamic claim to admire and respect Jesus (Isa) yet with a radically different perspective of his life's purpose.

Islamic statements regarding Jesus are minimalistic, yet stand in such contrast to Catholic revelation that they must be challenged and questioned in the public sphere.

Concurrently, increasing numbers of native born Australians are beginning to adopt aspects of Islamic tradition or to embrace outright conversion. Anecdotally, I have met a number of young Australians who have a strong perception that Islam offers a powerful sense of community, coupled with a decisive emphasis on family, children and extended family. This is often portrayed in stark contrast with Western community life which appears to be experiencing high divorce rates, undisciplined children and a de-emphasis on family. (particularly in contrast with individual rights). The intoxicating appeal of lifestyle security should not be underestimated in an Australian community which experiences divorce rates of 50 per cent.

One notable area of high Islamic conversion rates is in Australian prisons. These converts highlight a feeling of betrayal and abandonment from the wider society and note that Islamic discipline and structure help in adapting to prison conditions.

In essence it may be that the Islamic appeal is limited to specific sections of Australian society, particularly those damaged by lack of family and community and seeking stability in these areas.

Research from the University of Wales conducted in 2007 calculated that around 5,200 British convert to Islam each year and that the total convert number across the United Kingdom has reached 100,000. In the USA, a 2007 PEW Research poll estimated American Muslims at 2.4 million with approximately one quarter of this number being converts. Australian figures are not available but anecdotal evidence suggests conversion to Islam is a developing phenomenon. Notwithstanding the Islamic appeal to some sections of the Australian community, the Church needs to reinforce and clarify its basic teachings, especially its claims about Jesus and the centrality of his life for all humanity. The Australian tendency to see Jesus as a "good bloke", but removed from his salvific or healing role, contributes to a public perception of the "dumbed down" Jesus as little different from Islamic portrayals and without any lasting or universal significance.

The unique identity of Jesus is not evident in Koranic portrayals of his life. Certainly, the Koran speaks of Jesus with respect, yet ordinarily adds descriptors to confirm that he is merely another man: "Jesus is no more than a mortal whom we favoured and proposed as an instance of divine power to the children of Israel" (*Sura* 43.60). In another Koranic verse, Muhammad rejects Christ's claim that he is equal with his father and that the father and he are one:

> It is not right for a man that God should give him the scriptures and the wisdom, and the gift of prophecy and that he should then say to his followers "Be ye worshippers of me, as well as of God" (*Sura* 3. 73-74).

In this Koranic understanding of Jesus, the Incarnation, the Christ who comes to us as Emmanuel at Christmas is firmly denied. Within Islamic theology the idea of God's total transcendence precludes any possibility of God coming amongst us. For Islam God remains an unrivalled figure and all humanity remains only as part of the created order.

Jesus is not depicted as a pre-eminent prophet in the Koran and his place alongside other prophets is negligible. Moses, for example, has a far more profound status and Muhammad's position as the final prophetic witness is stressed at every opportunity.

Muhammad's night journey is an important Islamic tradition which recounts his dream journey to paradise, through seven levels of heaven into the presence of God. This story is recorded in all of the major strands of Hadith, a series of traditions about the life of Muhammad considered to be normative for Muslims. This traditional story suggests a more prominent role for Moses (encountered in sixth heaven) and Abraham (encountered in seventh heaven) than Jesus (second heaven) who meets Muhammad at the beginning of his journey towards God.

The reality of the status of the Koranic Jesus is best summed up in *Sura* 4 (169-172):

> O people of the book! Do not overstep the bounds of your Religion; do not utter lies against God and speak only truth. The Messiah, Jesus, son of Mary is only a messenger of God. His word, which he sent down to Mary and a spirit from him. Therefore, believe in God and his messengers and do not say three. Desist it is better for you. God is only one. Far be it from him that he should have a son! To him belongs what is on heaven and earth. God is sufficient for a protector.

These verses are clearly addressed to Christians, and plainly reject Christian Trinitarian revelation, the divinity of Jesus and consequently any need for faith in Christ as a necessity for salvation.

The Koran with its unbending individualism holds that each human is responsible before God on the day of Judgement. Conceptions of God as a merciful advocate, as intercessor for humanity, of divine *kenosis* (self-emptying) in partnership with humanity are completely absent from both the Koran and Hadith.

The Koran's purpose in placing Jesus within the prophetic sequence is essentially to discredit Christian teachings of Christ's divinity, his resurrection and his salvation of all humanity. Islam is unable to accept any notion of Christ's redemptive death, his resurrection or his eternal partnership with humanity. *Sura* 4 (157) states again:

> Verily we have slain the messiah, Jesus, the son of Mary, a messenger of God. Yet, they slew him not, and they crucified him not, but they only thought they did.

With these challenging Islamic views of Jesus, Catholicism has an important matter to consider. How do we regard the question of Christ to his disciples, "Who do you say I am?" (Matt 16.15). Is this a universal question and is there a Catholic obligation to put this question to all people in all ages?

Additionally, the Islamic viewpoint also brings into clarity the direct commandment of Jesus to "go and make disciples of all nations". In the tradition of the Catholic Church and the witness of the Gospel accounts the uniqueness of Jesus is paramount, as Christ himself affirms:

> The Spirit of the Lord is upon me because he has anointed me to preach good news to the poor. He has sent me to proclaim release to the captives and recovery of sight to the blind, to set at liberty those who are oppressed, to proclaim the acceptable year of the Lord (Luke 4:18-19).

Further Reading

John Esposito, *The Future of Islam*, Oxford University Press, 2010.

A. Guillaume, *The Life of Muhammad*, Oxford University Press, 2002.

S.S. Hassan, *Christians versus Muslims in Modern Egypt*, Oxford University Press, 2003.

Jytte Klausen *The Islamic Challenge: Politics and Religion in Western Europe*, Oxford University Press, 2008.

Robert Reilly, *The Closing of the Muslim Mind: How Intellectual Suicide Created the Modern Islamist*, ISI Books, 2010.

Bat Ye'or, *The Decline of Eastern Christianity under Islam*, Fairleigh Dickinson University Press, 1996.

Bat Ye'or, *The Dhimmi: Jews and Christians Under Islam*, Fairleigh Dickinson University Press, 1985.

7

CATHOLICISM AND BEAUTY

Beauty

Beauty has traditionally been counted amongst the ultimate values of Western civilisation, along with, truth, goodness and justice. The concept of beauty as an objective quality has also been central to Catholic understandings of art, music, architecture, love and sacrifice, but most importantly of the human soul. For Catholics, beauty is a wonderful gift from God to humanity, as it speaks of the nature of God himself.

When we apprehend beauty with our hearts we are also led to the reality of a spiritual life with Christ and a life beyond ourselves. Our modern society is largely shaped by the crass and short-lived fads of popular culture and celebrity promoted by the mass media. In much of the Western world and in most of our cities there is a profound lack of beauty as functionalism and financial considerations rule all. In our cultural sphere, the antics of sporting figures and celebrities have taken the place of love and beauty in our own lives and relationships. Our sense of wonder and awe is trumped by lowest common denominators in behaviour and intellect but most importantly our sense of soul is ignored or rubbished as not required in love or sacrifice.

The British philosopher Roger Scruton comments in his work *Beauty* (OUP, 2009) on our current circumstances: "Beauty is downgraded as something too sweet, too escapist, and too far from realities to deserve our undivided attention." Certainly, there are strong impulses within our society which seek to reject and denigrate convictions that home, peace, faith and contentment are worthy or seminal. Indeed these truths are often portrayed as lies needing to give way to the "real truth" of our grubby, shallow and unfulfilling human condition.

Naturally, the Catholic Church stands against such a psychological and spiritually destructive view of humanity. In Catholic theology, the world is fallen, yet its redemption and ultimate destination has already been revealed. Hence, the Church opposes a view of humanity that suggests things are hopeless, futile or unchangeable. The missionary, charity and social justice works of the Catholic Church speak profoundly of her belief in the full-redemption of humanity.

Of particular concern for the Church throughout her history has been the beauty and peace to be found in her cathedrals, parishes and liturgies. This has never been (as is sometimes portrayed in modern times) a self-indulgent desire to demonstrate or flaunt wealth or power. Certainly, Catholic worship can take place in a tin shed but as any musical beginner knows, what we strive for and what we try to realise is the fullness, beauty and richness of a Beethoven or Mozart. As we enter into the wonder, complexity and beauty of the masterpiece, so in the cathedrals and churches we see and touch something of the depth, awe and love of the Trinity.

In recent times, Catholicism has also been challenged by many, both within and without, to change, modernise or somehow adapt to the tasks and expectations of the modern "secularised" Catholic. In my view we have gone too far in this accommodation. Indeed, much of what is wheeled out in many Catholic parishes, musically, in homily, or in liturgical practice is often little more than dross. The banal, unsingable and repetitive chorus not only fails to lift the spirits of the faithful but actually messages the idea that church leaders are more out of touch than ever before. The modernist priest has often only ensured that the beauty of the Mass has become empty, repetitious, mechanical and cliché ridden. As a result such priests are only succeeding in emptying their buildings.

It is also the case that many modern parish churches have failed to inspire. Naturally, it is difficult to imagine that dual purpose structures or churches that resemble community halls could do anything else but encourage locals to conclude that the truth, beauty and awe of the faith is superfluous. In the early decades of the 21st century, we must ensure that the search for Our Lord and his love and beauty can be seen and experienced in our churches. Dumbing-down our architecture, homilies and liturgy does nothing except hasten Catholic decline and irrelevance in Australia.

Our contemporary culture has also spawned many artistic, musical, radio and television performances that are not only ugly, but through a desire for "newness" and "relevance" manage to spoil beauty. The footballer who sees no problem in "drinking his own urine" or the cricketer who displays his texting infidelity with pride do more than undermine their sports. They suggest and highlight an inner world with nothing beyond itself. Catholicism must vigorously oppose such a narrow and soulless public world. Ensuring the awe-inspiring beauty of our parishes and Mass is an essential starting point. Catholicism must again offer a vision of life beyond contemporary social norms. Junk music and folksy homilies have converted no-one and left the faithful cold and disillusioned.

A love of beauty is intrinsic to a fulfilled human life. Without the ability to appreciate beauty, to seek beauty in our lives and to see our Catholic vocation as revealing beauty to others we risk a diminished, alienated or resentful life that is lived remote from a community or society of nurture and compassion. Australia already has too many young people let down by our education system, who leave school not only without basic education skills but, more importantly, are unable culturally or ascetically to participate fully in our society.

I am a great lover of the Australian sports psychology and the tribalism and enthusiasm of many sporting associations, but I do not wish for a society in which our predominant "role model" or major interests are centred on the self-destruction of our newest sports star.

The Catholic Church spends a great deal of time and energy in the alleviation of poverty. This is good and powerful work, nevertheless we must also ensure that the ignorant, crass and boorish are also able to be drawn into another world beyond the limitations of their current lives. There is no other organisation in the Western world that is capable of such work. If not the Catholic Church then who can concentrate a spotlight on the presence of something more significant than our current popular culture with its deficient and vulgar interests and desires?

The condition of Australian culture and Western civilisation is impoverished but not yet completely in ruin. I have encountered many young Australians who believe falsely that Australian culture and society have nothing to offer them, yet their experience of a life beyond their immediate world is token at best. These young Australians cry out for something more from our society, but due to their limited exposure to mainstream values are unable to envision a world that actually offers a beneficial future.

A Catholic emphasis on beauty and culture must have as a crucial goal the raising of aspirations in an endeavour to re-engage Australian life in learning to appreciate moral values, religious precepts, love of beauty, respect for others and a renewed desire for self-improvement. This will require a substantial change in the Church from seeing itself as a remnant community in an increasingly barbarian sea to a community that is charged with change and understands itself as the crucial institution in fulfilling this change.

Western societies, including Australia, currently have a heavy emphasis on rights, which in practice allow an individual to pursue activities that focus completely on the self as long as no other individuals are harmed or disadvantaged. Such an intense priority towards the individual has ensured that increasingly Australians are manifesting a wide-range of addictive behaviours.

Modern Australia is confronting increased levels of substance abuse, alcohol and drug related disorders, a vast increase in depression and higher suicide rates, particularly amongst young men. These long-standing difficulties now find themselves merged with a new brand of Western problems, focusing on the social aspects of culture. Cyber bullying, sex addiction, anxiety disorders, hoarding, and on-line shopping addictions all point to a breach in the public and private worlds. The emergence of Facebook has seen thousands of individuals post their most intimate thoughts on others, or photos of private behaviour, no longer understanding the personal and social costs of such activities. Ironically, the more we seem connected in these "pseudo" ways, the greater the sense of loneliness and alienation. These individuals, who seek recognition in the most disconnected of ways, all display one strong characteristic: they lack genuine community. It is here that the Church's great call to mission must be directed.

Here there are a number of attributes to our dysfunctional modern Australia that can be transformed, if Catholicism is able to grasp this necessity in terms of a cultural and spiritual mission. The lack of appreciation of beauty amongst younger Australians inhibits them from undertaking experiences that push them "beyond themselves". Without these "beyond themselves" moments, they are locked into an individual world where the "ego" is all. From here it is not far to experiences that are only self-orientated and still only a small further step to the inability to connect with others, to value community and ultimately to turn on both self and society. Without an inner world that can appreciate, art, beauty, faith and Western culture we create individuals who leap from one stimulus to another without ever learning to love, to hope, or to see beyond the immediate "me" experience. Within a wider historical context, many look at the

Roman Colosseum which exhibited forms of entertainment focused on violence, humiliation and deliberate murder (all for general public consumption) and wonder how this society with an emphasis on law, beauty and architectural excellence could produce such an anomaly.

Yet, modern Australia is also confronted with a similar set of anxieties. We have amplified a society in which the need for stimulation has encouraged local television to portray overweight individuals or those competing for cooking, musical or house building prizes, in deliberate stress and conflict situations for public entertainment. Good taste or sophistication is rarely present in any of our popular television, radio or internet offerings.

Many Australians answer surveys suggesting that despite material wealth they are deeply unhappy. Is it unreasonable to suggest that our popular culture, which offers nothing of lasting value, should be linked to a society that is deeply unhappy. In these circumstances, Catholicism needs to provide television, radio and internet programs, under its own control, that offer alternatives to the current witless drivel.

If the Church cannot offer a visible and popular form of entertainment that revives aesthetic appreciation, then we can expect more addicted forms of behaviour and wasted lives.

In many ways our popular culture reflects a heartless world in which superficial stereotypes allow us in one moment to perform shallow hero worship and in the next to tear down and destroy such figures. This paradigm is seen most clearly in our relationship to sporting figures. The ongoing Essendon Football Club drug allegations saga highlights what a manipulated public should expect to see.

Accused former superstars and current coaches such as James Hird and Mark Thompson are expected to make public mea culpa for alleged misdeeds in compliance or failure to care for their players. Through an aggressive and bullying media, these coaches are expected to undertake public apologies or risk having their reputations destroyed, to accept sanctions without any evidence or proof of guilt. These individuals are subsequently scapegoated to convince the wider society and a football community that potential problems are under control and that the evils of drugs in sport are being confronted.

The difficulty of such demands from a shallow public is that individuals who feel themselves innocent, such as Hird and Thompson, are subsequently labelled as "bringing the game into disrepute", a catch-all phrase in which nothing actually changes, and no real problem solving takes place.

In our current "public sphere" the role of the court system is replaced by sports journalists such as Caroline Wilson and Patrick Smith whose expertise in sport is minimal but who act as moral guardians for popular culture. I have no knowledge of the individuals concerned but do highlight the reality that a society which conducts its witch-hunts in public, that expects the accused to quickly repent publicly and that punishes via "vague disrepute provisions" is not actually moral, transparent or forgiving. All that has changed is that public entertainment is now given a moral veneer.

The process of establishing guilt, of personal and private forgiveness, and of absolution is no longer a functioning reality, but a game to be manipulated within a predominately ugly society. There is no morality in this process, only damaged and hurt individuals, as meanwhile the media caravan moves on seeking the next victim.

This modern day process can also be glimpsed in the 2014 case of Georgian Opera singer Tamar Iveri. Opera Australia terminated her contract after she had written an openly anti-gay letter to the Georgian President. I am not suggesting that this behaviour is cultured or worthy of support, nevertheless the judgement of an artist by entirely non-artistic criteria sets an impoverished precedent. This harassment of a woman who holds a non-politically correct opinion, offers no ability for reflection, developed understanding or meaningful life change. No doubt, she will soon issue a "heartfelt" apology and get on with her career, but more importantly changes in Australian culture and thinking should now be noted. The guise of moralism is really just a form of intolerance, deceitfully dressed up as caring. The intolerance shown towards Tamar Iveri differs little from her own views on homosexuals, with such behaviour distracting a shallow society from the real business of mature discussion and growth.

Beauty and faith are calls to our higher nature, symbolising two sides of the same coin. For Catholics love and affection between people are valuable only to the extent that they lead to self-sacrifice for others. It is in this action that true beauty is found. This is the reason the Church creates saints, in order to show the connection between love and sacrifice. The beauty of liturgy, art, music or literature illustrates the same connection. The Church's role is to present this bond as God's great gift to humanity, given that within modern Australia, the connection between beauty and our culture is ruptured.

We live as if beauty does not matter at all while we have mostly lost the idea of self-sacrifice and service to others. When Jesus confronted Satan during the temptation in the wilderness, he was offered the riches of the world, if he would only bow down and worship Satan. His response was that "man does not live on bread alone". This remains the great challenge for modern Australia. We have the freedom to despise the world, our fellow humans and even ourselves, but there is another way. This path leads from self-hatred towards the sacred and sacrificial. Catholicism has never been more counter-cultural than it is today in regard to modern Australia.

Further Reading

Roger Scruton, *Beauty – A very Short Introduction*, Oxford University Press, 2009.

8

CATHOLICISM AND THE ECONOMY

A Catholic Moral Position on the Economy

The Australian economy faces a number of significant challenges in the coming decades. Many of these will be shared by Western economies throughout the world, particularly those who have in recent times being unable to restrain government spending and have subsequently high debt to savings ratios.

The Australian recession of 1974 saw unemployment rise to 6.8 per cent and was followed by six years of deficit budgets amounting to a culmination deficit of 7.9 per cent of GDP. The 1990-1992 recession produced unemployment rates of up to 11 per cent and drove accumulation deficit to 17.2 per cent of GDP. Following the recent 2007-2009 Global Financial Crisis, currently both major Australian political parties are working on the assumption of a new cumulative deficit by 2017 of 20.5 per cent of GDP. The recent tendency of Australian governments to fail to balance the books is expected to see the national debt increase from $360 billion in 2014 to $450 billion by 2017.

This is a serious moral question for Australians given the now obvious reality that we have effectively passed payment for today's spending onto our children and grandchildren. Additionally, our ability to control and modify our economy will be severely restrained by debt repayment that will impact most severely on two major areas of Catholic concern, the unemployment rate and those individuals and families unable to adjust to changing circumstances and who suffer long-term disadvantage.

Government policies in recent years have dramatically increased welfare spending, including a striking increase in middle-class benefits and family support. Moreover, recent adjustments to labour markets including high minimum wages, coupled with a weakening of regulatory oversight allowing some trade unions to increase secondary boycotts, have significantly increased Australian business costs.

This has resulted in greater difficulty for the young to commence employment and for the unemployed (particularly those over 55) to re-enter the workplace. Nevertheless, it is not clear why Australians have become increasingly wedded to welfare spending, with a greater focus on the concerns of the present at the expense of the future.

There are a number of possible reasons for Australian indifferent economic management of recent years.

Australians have always prided themselves on their nation's egalitarian foundation and the continued reality of a relatively fair, equitable and financially balanced society. Australians have traditionally prided themselves on the middle-class nature of their society and most importantly on the absence of any significant financial underclass. However, this has changed over the past 30 years. We now have for the first time in our history a substantial number of individuals who are completely ill-equipped to effectively participate in Australian life. These deficiencies are educational, cultural, religious and psychological. Increasingly, in all of our major cities we have developed an inter-generational failure which sees many suburbs lacking any effective fathering, few family members with any work experience, poor quality schools, and limited job opportunities. An entitlement welfare culture prevails along with a psychological hostility towards outside forces which includes authorities that may work in these areas (police, teachers, etc.) but also extends to a disrespect and lack of identification with wider Australia.

Within this picture, there is tribalism in many forms including football clubs, bikie-gangs and ethnic heritage as the key elements of identity and recently an attachment to Islamic teachings that downplay loyalty to Australia's norms and values.

The reality is that the nation, its language, culture, laws and values are all things that Australians share. If we allow aspects of these unifying factors to be subverted we are all diminished, as we create increasing numbers of people who "physically" live in Australia but don't feel they belong, or even have no wish to do so.

Inevitably, all Australians will dislike certain aspects of our society and may wish to reform them. I am one of them, having no love for the arrogant behaviour, alcoholism and disrespect for local culture shown by many Australians while travelling in Asian regions like Bali or Thailand. Nevertheless, this aversion to some aspects of Australian life should not cause us to despise those individuals but to seek their reform and improvement.

Furthermore, we should not conceal that reality by pouring money into organisations that do not concentrate on unifying our society but whose actual agenda is more likely to keep this disunity in place.

The welfare lobby regularly misrepresents the causes of issues such as unemployment but also advocates for solutions that do little to alleviate poverty. Indeed, it often pursues policies that deny jobs to the poor. The indigenous lobby is sometimes wedded to a socialist-community model of Aboriginal culture that is long gone and often seeks to downplay the value of private property, work incentives and the importance of school attendance. The environmental lobby exaggerates the harm done by new technologies such as shale fracking, so allowing Australian energy needs and costs to spiral without offering alternatives apart from the non-economic solar and wind technologies. This lack of attention to the primary issues of the emergence of Australian "tribalism" and the lack of solutions to proposals other than failed socialist ones, means that we will continue to spend huge amounts of financial resources on areas that remain "black holes".

The successful Chinese "capitalist" model offers us some incentive, that it is possible to rehabilitate failed regions through increasing investment in actual "real" businesses, and encouraging private ownership and serious access to markets at home and abroad. The low rates of unemployment are a key element in the defeat of tribal tendencies in Australia. Another is the strengthening of Catholic education and community life, with the emphasis on the universality of faith as distinctive from tribal allegiance.

Australian institutions in the last thirty to forty years have undergone a period of profound change. Unfortunately, what has happened broadly to all of these institutions has been an increase in public disrespect, cynicism and lack of trust.

Police, teachers, priests, government workers and, most importantly, politicians are often treated with cynicism or disrespect, with many Australians viewing them as fundamentally dishonest and as no longer serving the interests of all Australians. This change can be shown within these professions by the increasingly high turnover of membership and the increase of ill-health related to stress and depression. The dissatisfaction within some professions often means that these organisations are in permanent recruiting mode, constantly losing good people prior to completion of reasonable service and without enough quality people ascending to leadership roles.

Recently, the Australian Defence Force, Catholic clergy, the Salvation Army and medical professionals have all been subjected to extensive and emotional media treatment, particularly around sexual abuse or bullying.

These are difficult areas, with the media playing an essential investigative role. Nevertheless, many of these "revelations" of improper conduct do prove to be baseless and press judgements of guilt or innocence often prove false. The Australian Broadcasting Commission has done little credit to the Australian navy through its continued broadcasting of allegations of brutality made by asylum seekers which subsequently prove to be false. A willingness to rush to judgement further discredits the work of our service personnel and does little to affirm the profound societal contribution our military provides. This tendency in the media is not helpful or appropriate and contributes to the general background disrespect towards our institutions which has now strongly taken hold in some Australian minds.

Arguably, Australia's institutions are at their lowest ebb since Federation and our generalised lack of respect for authority does nothing to strengthen our community life as a whole. Attitudes that settle within Australian public life which effectively suggest that a "trust no-one" view is an effective way to relate to the wider society are bound to deflate and depersonalise those who hold them. The irony of Australian life is that the more we cry out for government to "do something" the greater the number of our fellow Australians who expect nothing and have descended into parochialism.

Many organisations are vulnerable to corruption, lacking a vision of their work and purpose and being distracted into fulfilling "catchphrases" without undertaking the hard decisions that will produce long-term benefits.

The Catholic Church is not immune from this phenomenon. Naturally we must ensure that our institutions are continually strengthened to resist corruption and to remove those guilty of corrupt behaviour. Rightly, community anger against the Catholic Church is not only directed at paedophile priests but more importantly at decision making further up the chain of command that failed to take appropriate action, either through ignorance or deceit. Unless institutions can quickly and efficiently remove those members of staff found to have acted corruptly or criminally, the long haul of regaining community trust cannot begin. Institutions, which do not constantly undertake internal reform, are bound to remain short-sighted, self-indulged and lacking in big picture or long term goals. We are all diminished by such reactionary institutions. The Catholic Church can and does play an essential role in this strengthening process. Indeed, the shock of clergy abuse and the subsequent loss of standing for the Church, including in the eyes of those who have lost faith and stopped attending Mass, indicate the high status Catholicism formerly occupied and which it needs to regain quickly. Importantly, Catholics must focus on the core issues confronting our society and not the marginal "wedge" social issues that arise from time to time, but which are not essential to the functioning of our society. Australians constantly suggest in opinion polls that issues such as same sex marriage, illegal refugee arrivals and climate change are not core issues during election periods, important though they may be to some Australians in the short-term.

Overwhelmingly, Australians point to a series of core economic considerations and concerns they expect our key institutions, (including the Church) to address. The general fate of the economy is our greatest priority including issues of unemployment, national debt, health care, petrol prices, budget deficits and education which continue to be uppermost in the minds of most Australians. This has been the same general list of priorities throughout our history. In recent times (post 9/11) terrorism has entered the Australian psyche as another essential concern. Without doubt, these polls indicate a desire from a large majority of Australians to continue to protect our economic strength, lifestyle and shared values.

Unfortunately, a number of Australian churches, including the Anglican and Uniting churches, tend to focus attention on the peripheral issues such as gay marriage, climate change and refugee policy, at the same time, these churches have nothing to say on the central economic concerns of modern Australians. In witnessing the dramatic demise of these churches, their lack of relevance, and poor economic policy credentials, the Catholic Church must ensure it does not proceed down this same populist path. The strength of any institution comes from continual working and reworking of its "core values" and the modern presentation of these principles and ethical standards.

How can the Catholic Church support underlying moral economic values?

Of central economic concern for Catholics must be the retention of the fundamental Australian idea that economic progress will benefit not just contemporary Australians, but future ones as well. We have throughout our history been a country that supports egalitarianism while seeking a better future for our children and grandchildren. This is an important principle as it fosters a commitment to shared values today which can be maintained and passed on to future generations.

Consequently, poor economic growth not only leads to diminished prosperity, but also ensures that inadequate infrastructure and a lack of consistent investment and sustained business development deliver a poorer future for all. Of particular concern for Catholics, given Christ's love of the poor and the outsider, is that non-growth or low growth both disadvantage poorer Australians, and continue to foster inequality throughout society. Australia's economic growth rate from 2010-2014 has hovered between one and three per cent which is insufficient to meet the infrastructure and investment needs of the nation. While Australia enjoys a comparative economic advantage in resources and primary products other service sectors such as tertiary education, medical facilities and tourism industries are greatly challenged by the emerging Asian markets. Indeed the provisions of medical and dental services in Asia are now having a substantial impact on the Australian domestic market. To maintain current standards of living and to continue to help the disadvantaged in our community, Australia needs regular growth at around four per cent of GDP.

Australian governments must pursue, and the Catholic Church must support, policies that contribute to increased growth in the Australian economy.

Philosophically, there are two strategies that have been advanced as to the best method of stimulating economic growth. In one method, the state plays the primary role. This model advocates high levels of government spending, dramatically increased levels of borrowing on currency markets (resulting in greater debt) and high taxation to pay for this stimulus and borrowing. During the Rudd Government of 2007-2010, a series of economic stimulus packages were implemented which focused on a one-off payment of $900 to each working Australian (total $12.7 billion), an educational building program for schools infrastructure ($14.7 billion) and free installation of insulation and solar water rebates ($3.9 billion). The short-term result of this stimulus regime was that Australia technically avoided recession but in the long term it severely restricted the ability of future governments of both persuasions to advance their own programs for Australian prosperity (due to high levels of new debt).

The second method of economic growth concentrates on the development of free enterprise. This system is almost the exact opposite of state dominated economic models. Here an emphasis on support for entrepreneurs, the formation of new privately owned companies and the expansion of existing private businesses results in less government spending and borrowing, reduces private and company taxation and eases restrictive regulations on start-up businesses and excessive compliance on existing small to medium companies.

Since 2007 only the first of these economic strategies has been pursued. Meanwhile the current economic stagnation and low levels of consumer confidence suggest this economic approach is not working.

Progressively, the Australian economy has also been subjected to a significant increase in onerous regulations affecting a wide-range of business interests. On a local level this can be seen in our pubs, clubs and restaurants which are often unable to open on weekends or public holidays, due to recently initiated high penalty rates. The restaurant and catering industry turns over some $16 billion per annum while employing large numbers of casual and part-time workers. The outcome of such acute wage costs is that businesses are closed on weekends and reluctant to take on large numbers of younger first-time workers.

The Australian Industry Group has undertaken extensive surveys of the effects of regulation on Australian business. The average business spends almost four per cent of total annual expenditure on complying with regulations. This figure is high by world-standards. Nevertheless, most of these costs do not result in increased government funds as 80 per cent of total compliance costs are made to external providers such as legal and accounting firms.

Undoubtedly, the considerable increase in business regulation under the Rudd and Gillard governments has acted as a barrier to future growth and innovation. More importantly, from a Catholic theological and moral perspective, these regulations work against the employment of new staff and the reduction of unemployment, particularly for those over 55 or seeking their first job. Youth unemployment is not alleviated when compliance and regulatory considerations are onerous.

The Catholic Church should have a strong moral incentive to advocate the removal of unnecessary business regulations as well as the uneven application and the duplication which is also prevalent.

Immigration, particularly skilled immigration has been and remains an essential component of the future success of the Australian economy. Without skilled immigrants arriving and staying in Australia it is difficult to generate and maintain economic productivity.

The training and re-training of native born Australians is an essential element of our economic prosperity, yet we should also remember that research conclusively links the arrival of each new skilled immigrant with the creation and development of almost three jobs for local born Australians. Significant damage to our economic stability is created when false statements and popular misunderstandings suggest that migration impacts negatively on local employment prospects. The opposite is true, as skilled migrants create more jobs for the native born, as well as stimulating economic growth and prosperity.

Catholicism has an essential interest in the process of job creation for all Australians. And skilled immigration is an important component of our future economic success and should be supported.

An obsessive concentration on welfare solutions can blind committed Catholics to the fact that employment and prosperity often rely on free-market solutions, which in no shape or form should be dismissed as unbridled capitalism.

The Church's primary concern must be the alleviation of unemployment and under-employment, and the provision of meaningful jobs for young Australians commencing their working lives. This position connects strongly with Catholic social teaching. Unemployment robs people of their fundamental dignity and potential fulfilment and is especially harmful to the poor and the young. It also produces a potentially lasting blockage to the commencement of many valuable individual and community goals which Catholicism stresses as essential to the well-being of humanity, the pursuit of education, the freedom of love in marriage and the desire to nurture new life in the gift of children. These goals, which the Church sees as essential to Catholic family and social life, are already under considerable strain from rampant individualism. We do not need an additional burden that discourages young Australians.

I would suggest strongly that Australian Catholics consider both a diocesan and parish based response to unemployment, one that utilises our developing business network and the community reach of parish life. Some initial work has now commenced through the CYA Project (www.cyaproject.org) under the umbrella of the Catholics in Business network (www.catholicsinbusiness.org).

Catholic theological reflection in the papal encyclical of Pope Leo XIII (*Rerum Novarum*) supports and upholds this effective approach to unemployment:

> It is surely undeniable that, when a man engages in remunerative labour, the compelling reason and motive of his work is to obtain property, and therefore to hold it as his very own. If one man hires out to another his strength or skill, he does so for the purpose of receiving in turn what is necessary for the satisfaction of his needs, he therefore expressly intends to acquire a right, full and real, not only to the remuneration, but also to the disposal of such remuneration just as he pleases. Thus, if he lives sparingly, saves money, and, for greater security, invests his savings in land, the land, in such case, is only his wages under another form; and consequently, a working man's little estate thus purchased should be as completely at his full disposal as are the wages he receives for his labour. But it is precisely in such power of disposal that ownership obtains, whether the property consists of land or chattels. Socialists therefore, by endeavouring to transfer the possessions of individuals to the community at large, strike at the interests of every wage earner, since they would deprive him of the liberty of disposing of his wages, and thereby all hope and possibility

of increasing his resources and of bettering his condition in life (*Rerum Novarum*, p. 5).

Rerum Novarum makes the authentic connection between the pursuit of wages and the workers' important right of liberty in the disposal of their wealth and resources. For Catholicism, this has always been the essential route to self-improvement and community strength. *Rerum Novarum* could not foresee the current policies of many Western nations, including Australia, which restrict the ability of companies to hire new labour, through excessive regulation, complex and high company tax and the tendency of state bureaucracy to distort employment through increased public sector growth furthering more regulation and oversight. The clear losers in this economic model remain the unemployed, the over 55s and young first job seekers. Here the moral case and base teaching of the Church support a greater emphasis on reducing excessive regulation and company taxation and encouragement of the expansion of private enterprise and hence further job creation.

Australian governments of recent years have also followed another widespread Western economic impulse, the tendency to favour allegedly future "winner" industries over established business. This has commonly taken the form of industry subsidies for enterprises of uncertain commercial value. The most common expression of the substandard model within Australia have been the generous subsidies for environmental industries promising thousands of new "green jobs".

The American economist, Bryan Caplan, argues that the Australian public display a number of economic pre-dispositions: frequently an anti-market attitude combined with anti-foreign convictions; a general tendency to pessimism; and a recently acquired idea that government must provide employment for current and future generations. The promise of endless future "green jobs" taps into such inclinations, yet these initiatives actually diminish employment in the wider economy by diverting profitable investment into subsidising non-financially viable activities. This may be the first time in our economic history that the federal government has explicitly proposed policies that will make the economy less efficient. Renewable energy sources can be appropriate in some applications, yet they are decades away from competitive pricing and reliability for the base load requirements of a first world economy. The Catholic Church has a critical moral case to argue for the retention and development of meaningful employment in viable industries and not see government further distress working Australians with ideological delusions that produce no net increase in employment. There is a significant moral case for Catholics to promote the abandonment of all subsidies to industry as a fundamental cause of ineffectual job creation and a barrier to young Australians entering the workforce.

In private life, citizens are expected to manage and direct their finances in such a way as to provide for themselves and their families along with some provision for future needs. *Rerum Novarum* identifies these behaviours as fundamental requirements for human fulfilment.

Indeed, individuals who fail to fulfil or are distracted from this fundamental task are not seen as pulling their own weight, or as "bludging" on the wider society. While support should be extended to those trapped in poverty through birth, misfortune or the corruption of others, this should not extend to those who refuse to help themselves. As Scripture reminds us:

> For even when we are with you, we used to give you this order: If anyone is not willing to work, then he is not to eat either. For we hear that some among you are leading an undisciplined life, doing not work at all, but acting like busybodies. Now such persons we commend and extort in the lord Jesus Christ to work in quiet fashion and eat their own bread (2 Thessalonians 3:10-12).

If this is the Catholic reality for the individual, why is this not a similar moral issue for the state? Certainly in recent years, the crises in Greece and other European nations have drawn strong international criticism. Plainly, Greece and others have lived beyond their means for decades, relying on current consumption and excessive government spending. While the world is increasingly unwilling to extend further credit, it does nothing to consider the moral or theological perspective of trading our own comfort against the future of our children.

Australia has in recent years also conducted itself in a careless financial manner with a series of spending schemes that have run up huge debt. Within the top seventeen IMF countries, Australia had the fastest growth in spending and the third highest growth in debt. Our debt currently stands at $350 billion, with projections suggesting a debt of $667 billion by 2023-2024.

This prompts a far-reaching moral question. What kind of society will we leave to our children? Will it be one of future generations saddled with a substantial debt that reduces living standards, education and employment opportunities, or one where our children experience the same possibilities Australians currently enjoy? The Catholic Church in Australia, with its fundamental concerns for the unemployed and poor, needs to engage with this question. In recent days, the Australian government has entered into a wide community discussion in relation to government payments and entitlements. This has generated a degree of community angst over the potential loss of individual and family benefits. Nevertheless, we should remember that millions of taxpayer dollars are transferred to industries that have not resulted in the strengthening, modernising or competitiveness of these industries. The Productivity Commission has identified a substantial number of sectors in the Australian business community where subsidies have become financially unsustainable as well as fundamentally unfair. It is immoral for today's generation not to make the necessary changes to improve workplace competitiveness and to receive subsidies to industries that will be paid for by our children.

It can be profoundly unethical to provide generous assistance to some industries and not to others. As Australian Senator Bridget McKenzie noted: "Governments have supported car manufacturing to the tune of about $10 billion over the last seven years, while agricultural subsidies remain very low compared to international standards."

Australian Catholics must be astute when considering these issues. Nevertheless, as British historian and economist Niall Ferguson noted in 2013: "The public debt of government around the world allows the current generation of voters to live at the expense of those too young to vote or as yet unborn." This situation also applies to the Australian workplace.

In 1375 the Islamic philosopher Ibn Khaldun commented: "At the beginning of the dynasty, taxation yields a large revenue from small assessments. At the end of the dynasty, taxation yields a small revenue from large assessments." Taxation should be regarded as a moral issue within the Australian economy as its growth can impact upon issues of fairness and the egalitarian nature of our society.

In 2013, Judith Sloan and Henry Ergas, economic writers with *The Australian*, noted that during the Rudd years, "tax hikes have proliferated, including the poorly conceived and even more poorly implemented changes to the fringe benefits tax, the increase in tobacco excise and a levy on bank deposits". Dr Julie Novak, from the Institute of Public Affairs, has also highlighted "the new width, depth and variety of taxation under Rudd". Over the past six years, a raft of new taxes, fees and charges were introduced, including new taxes on carbon dioxide emissions, coal, iron-ore and alcopops, as well as increased imposts on tobacco, ethanol, LPG, luxury cars, superannuation and income tax surcharges, and rising visa application fees. Taxpayers will also foot the bill for interest payments on Commonwealth Government debt, which increased from less than $4 billion in 2007-2008 to around $11 billion in 2011-2012. In the long run, the burden falls on taxpayers to pay the bill and clean up the mess that political spendthrifts and regulatory enthusiasts leave behind (*Australian Taxpayers Magazine*, August 2013). While the Catholic Church has traditionally supported measures to assist the unemployed, the poor and Indigenous Australians, the level of generalised taxation across the community has now reached a critical point where the impact on average working families has become severe.

In my view, taxation within the Australian economy is too high. John F. Kennedy famously said: "It is a paradoxical truth that tax rates are too high today and tax revenues are too low. The soundest way to raise the revenues in the long run is to cut the rates now." This is now the position the Australian Government should take.

Lowering personal income tax rates is critical to encouraging Australians to work and invest more, which correspondingly results in higher economic growth.

The future success of the Australian economy, the maintenance of individual opportunity and the reduction of unemployment are all areas of moral consideration for Australian Catholics. They deserve our full consideration.

Further Reading

James Allan, *Democracy in Decline*, McGill-Queens University Press, 2014.

John Micklethwait & Adrian Wooldridge, *The Fourth Revolution: The Global Race to Reinvent the State*, Penguin Press, 2014.

9

THE GREENS POLITICAL MOVEMENT

The Catholic Church in Australia is facing another challenge to its fundamental principles in the rise of the Green environmental movement. This challenge has been around for a number of decades yet is still largely unacknowledged for the serious threat and menace it poses to Catholic life in Australia. Much of this confusion over Green hostility to Catholicism is masked for Catholics by their own inherent desire to do the right thing for the environment alongside a longing to leave the beauty of Australia to our children and future generations.

It is salient for Catholics to recall that the Church has a precious and powerful 2,000-year-old teaching that has established a deep understanding of the love of God for humanity as well as for all of his created order. Profoundly, Genesis establishes that God is the creator of our universe ("In the beginning God created heaven and earth", Genesis 1:1) but that God also saw that it was good (I: 4, 10, 12, 21).

Catholicism rightly derives two important understandings from Genesis, firstly that God created things to be "good" and that this creation and goodness reflect something of his nature, generosity and grandeur, especially towards humanity. Psalm 8 captures something of this generosity:

> I look up at your heavens, shaped by your fingers, at the

moon and the stars you set firm – what is man that you spare a thought for him, or the child of Adam that you care for him. Yet, you have made him little less than a God, you have crowned him with glory and honour, you have made him lord of the works of your hand and put all things under his feet, sheep and cattle, all of them, even wild beasts, birds in the sky, fish in the sea, when he makes his way across the ocean – Lord our God how majestic is your name throughout the world.

This psalm also reveals our surprising role as custodians of God's creation, despite our own dependent position. The great tradition of St Francis of Assisi and his Franciscan followers has always emphasised the necessity to contemplate God for his creation and to give thanks for our part in it. For St Francis, and all Catholics, there is the call spiritually and physically to participate in the creation, in a way that is free and self-determining. For Catholics, the gift from God of our reason has also placed a moral responsibility on the nature of our care and engagement with God's creation. Hence, mankind's jurisdiction over God's creation is driven by the principle of service for the common good of other humans as well as respect for all of creation.

Nevertheless, Catholicism also recognises that our reason and freedom do not always lead us to good choices and that we are equally capable of profound evil and destruction. The *Catechism of the Catholic Church* sums up this situation:

> Man, tempted by the devil, let his trust in his creator die in his heart and abusing his freedom, disobeyed God's command. In that sin, man preferred himself to God and by that very act scorned him. He chose himself over and against God, against the requirement of his creaturely status and therefore against his own good. Created in a state of holiness, man was destined to be fully "divinised" by God in glory. Seduced

by the devil, he wanted to "be like God" but 'without God, before God, and not in accordance with God" (*Catechism of the Catholic Church*, 397-398).

This has always been the difficulty for humanity in respect to God's creation as we alone of all God's creatures have the willpower, the intelligence and the responsibility to care for God's universe. How we do that remains the issue. Catholicism clearly shows a way forward in service to humanity and a responsibility to act in ways that do not despoil the created order.

Catholicism has also linked and emphasised an important gift to humanity that enables us to care for the environment and for each other: that is, the gift of work. Here our work is tied to our abilities to create and to progress and consequently to make our world a better place in which to live, not only politically or financially but also environmentally.

Scripture relates that Adam and Eve tended the garden, that Cain practised agriculture and that Abel tended flocks. Jesus himself most likely supported himself through carpentry, the disciples were fishermen and St Paul a tentmaker. The link between work, creation, progress and improvement is accentuated in ways not found in any other faith.

In 1991 Pope John Paul II summed up the nature of our partnership with God and with our environment:

> The earth, by reason of its fruitfulness and its capacity to satisfy human need is God's first gift for the sustenance of human life. But the earth does not yield its fruits without a particular human response to God's gift, that is to say, without working. It is through work, that man, using his intelligence and exercising his freedom, succeeds in making the earth a fitting home (*Centesimus Annus*, p. 31).

Through this great Catholic tradition, the Western world

has continued to encourage discovery, creation and mechanical improvements. Most of the great early scientists such as Galileo and Newton were Christians who saw their works as ways of glorifying God and of serving and improving the human condition.

This Catholic tradition continues today. Recently Robert Bryce from the US Manhattan Institute has highlighted impressive changes to data storage capacities which now see an average smartphone carry 250 million times the data storage of Apollo 11, the 1969 spacecraft that took Armstrong and Aldrin to the Moon:

> Bryce argues that "a similar dynamic", making less do more, drives virtually every technological change that has created the modern world from cars and planes to advances in medicine, strategic metals and the Cloud. Technological innovation in short, has a particular character – a dynamic of improvement, that accelerates and amplifies while requiring less space and material and at a lower cost (Arthur Herman, *Wall Street Journal*, 24 July 2014).

Catholic theological tradition would regard this modern "innovation analysis" as consistent with God's gift to humanity of reason, logic and intelligence, for use and for work, in the improvement of the human environment.

The Catholic position therefore stands in radical contrast to that proposed by many Green groups which are overwhelmingly anti-technology, anti-development and consequently anti-humanity. In the Catholic understanding, Green fundamentalists are on the wrong side of history in denying God's gift to humanity of making us co-creators and ignoring the demonstrable ability of human technology to improve the lives of us all, without damaging the environment. Those who would drive humanity backwards by denying energy to businesses and families, who push up costs by ignoring shale fracking and drilling gas solutions, or improvements to clean nuclear energy, are simply wedded to an impoverished ideology that has never delivered practical results.

The modern concern for the environment came into sharp focus during the industrial revolution and the visual image of vast polluting smoke stacks dotted over landscapes, particularly in northern England.

Nevertheless, industrialisation and improved agricultural techniques have allowed more people to enjoy improved lives and acquire greater wealth than at any stage in human history. The working class has actually been the greatest beneficiary from these technological improvements. Advances in medicine have largely eliminated diseases such as smallpox, tuberculosis, malaria, polio and measles. Certainly, problems still remain with greenhouse gas emissions, mostly from coal burning, yet what is often forgotten is that this coal technology enabled us to move from the destructive wood-burning pollution of the past. The development of efficient electrical and gas heating in the 1950s ended the notorious London pea-soupers of the early 20th century. Contrary to popular opinion most Western nations have actually increased forest size and density over the last 100 years, although, unfortunately, there is a different story in the developing world where wood is still relied upon for heating. Environmentalists from Western nations who dissuade developing nations from pursuing technological improvements, such as electricity and gas production, actually disadvantage further the poorest of the world's populations, denying them the benefits enjoyed in Western nations.

The underlying philosophy of many Green activists is that humanity is not a particularly special or noteworthy species. Indeed some would even portray humanity as a cancer infecting the body of "mother earth". Nothing could be further opposed to the Catholic understanding that we are made in the "image and likeness of God" and endowed with special gifts of reason, intelligence and creativity.

The Church has historically encouraged the creativity and intelligence displayed in humanity. This encouragement has been across the whole spectrum of human activities: music, art, philosophy, science, economics and politics, even through to advances in manufacturing and automotive innovation. Through all of these innovations Catholicism encourages and supports the advancement of the human condition and the benefits this brings for all of God's creation.

Regrettably, the Green movement has also on occasions demonstrated an unreasonable aggression against private companies generating wealth through exploration and ongoing mining activity. On the other hand the Church takes the view that private freedom and responsiveness to commercial innovation lie at the heart of a just and equalitable distribution of benefits to all.

In *Centesimus Annus* Pope John Paul II reminds us that "the free market is the most efficient instrument for utilising resources and effectively responding to needs" (34). For Catholics, economic activity, including exploration and mining, are certainly another way humanity participates in the co-creation of a just and equitable world and an unspoiled environment.

For Catholics, environmental issues and economic benefits for humanity are conjoined issues. As Pope John Paul II has highlighted Catholics see democratic nations and free enterprise as more likely to respond to the preservation of the environment. The Church rejects the Green tendency to portray centrally planned government controlled actions as more environmentally responsible than privately owned institutions.

Pope John Paul II sums up well the Catholic stance on the environment: "Ecological responsibility cannot base itself on the rejection of the modern world or on the vague wish to return to a lost paradise" (*The Ecological Crisis*, 1989, 13). Rightly, the Church recognises that human jurisdiction over the environment is an ongoing responsibility but that our primary religious responsibilities are to be focused on loving God and our neighbours as ourselves (Luke 10:27).

The Australian environmental movement and pagan philosophies

In recent years it has become increasingly apparent to Catholics that the Australian environmental movement is not exclusively a scientifically based movement.

Tim Flannery, palaeontologist and global warming activist, was Australian of the Year in 2007 and Chief Commissioner of the government appointed Climate Commission from 2011 until its closure in September 2013.

While Flannery's publications have certainly raised the profile of environmental issues there are a number of aspects of his work which should raise concerns for both Catholics and other thinking Australians.

Flannery supports the GAIA principle which proposes that organisms interact with their inorganic surroundings to form self-regulating systems. This GAIA hypothesis lacks any evidential support and is not backed by either evolutionary theory or empirical evidence found in the geological record. Flannery explained his particular understandings of the GAIA hypothesis for the English *Guardian* newspaper: "For the first time, this global super-organism, this global intelligence will be able to send a signal, a strong and clear signal to the earth. And what that means in a sense is that we can, we will be regulating intelligence for the planet, I'm sure in the future." Flannery spoke in similar vein during the ABC *Science Show*. "This planet, this GAIA, will have acquired a brain and a nervous system. That will make it a living animal, a living organism."

James Paterson, director of development and communications at the Institute of Public Affairs has noted (*IPA Review*) some worrying authoritarian trends in both Flannery and other environmentalists. Paterson notes "prominent Green activists, Clive Hamilton, for instance, have suggested that the suspension of democratic processes might be a necessary 'emergency' response to the threat of climate change". *Sydney Morning Herald* columnist Elizabeth Farrelly recently wrote that "Australia's ludicrous dithering on a pollution tax" was evidence that voting should be a "privilege" rather than a right and that "China should be envied because it need not 'pander' to voters."

Paterson also pointed out that Flannery has warned Australians that "beaches are going to disappear with climate change" and that "eight storey buildings by a beach will have waves lapping their roofs". Paterson notes that current Bureau of Meteorology estimates predict 10mm rises per year suggesting that Flannery's alarmist predictions are thousands of years away! Flannery's dire predictions of severe drought and lack of water in Australia's largest cities have not eventuated. Not to be deterred, Flannery has suggested that floods and bushfires along with other extreme weather are more likely to occur through human-generated climate change.

That Pagan religious understandings should have penetrated so deeply into the environmental movement is perhaps surprising. Nevertheless there is nothing in the Catholic tradition to suggest that environmental advocacy should be at the expense of humanity, democracy or private industry. Nor does the Church suggest that imbuing the earth with intelligence, emotions or a moral ascendency over humanity is a helpful approach to the natural concern that many Catholics have for our nation's environment.

The Greens political party also has a number of policy statements that should be alarming to Catholics. While the Greens rightfully see education as a public good they seek to prioritise the public education system in ways that will cause significant detriment and impairment to Australia's private schools, of which Catholic schools form the largest cohort.

Article 4. 4A, 4B and articles 5 and 8 of the stated aims of the Green educational policy states the following:

4. Recognising that the substantial growth in federal funding to non-government schools has had an adverse impact on public education, any funding to non-government schools:

   (a) To be set so that total public subsidy to the non-government sector does not advantage private education at the expense of public education; and

   (b) To take into account the resources of each individual school, a direct measure of parental socio-economic status and the schools capacity to generate income from all sources, including fees and other contributions.

5. The money saved from ending the public funding of those very wealthy non-government schools, which would not receive funding under such a model, reinvested into public schools with the highest proportion of students from disadvantaged backgrounds.

6. The same accountability and transparency frameworks for public funding to be required of non-government schools as are required of government schools including

   (a) Non-discrimination in the hiring of staff;

   (b) Non-discrimination in the selection of students and an admission and expulsions policies similar to government schools, including an obligation to enrol; and

   (c) Provision of all information necessary to escalate the income the school has the capacity to generate from fees and all other sources.

There is little doubt in my mind that this educational policy amounts to a scheme of picking winners. Also inherent in this policy is a radical bias favouring government schools at the expense of private institutions.

Regrettably a latent hostility seems prevalent in Green opposition to private wealth and the notion that individuals or families can make choices to spend their money as they see fit. Hostility to private schooling (even wealthy schools) takes no account of the significant sacrifices that many parents make to maintain their children in these schools.

With the Australian Greens seemingly anti-individual and family choice, it is difficult not to see these policies, by extension as anti-Catholic. The reality of these policies is, if enacted, they would work significantly against families who wished their children to participate in faith-based education. Why should families of Catholic faith be discriminated against through financial pressure? Given that the Catholic education system is the largest provider of private education, to financially penalise these schools, or to paint them as especially privileged, takes no realistic account of Catholic school funding, nor of the hard working struggle of most Catholic parents to provide an education for their children.

The Australian Greens party seems subtly committed to an attack on religious freedom. Article 8 of its educational policy suggests that non-government schools (i.e., Catholic schools) would forfeit the right to hire or fire staff as they see fit. It follows that if staff, for whatever reason, were reluctant to follow Catholic values and practices, the school would be deprived the right to remove them. This can only ensure that over time Catholic values, beliefs and practices would be weakened or even disappear. What is the point of a Catholic school, unable to adhere to and teach its unique Catholic identity? Such a school would soon be indistinguishable from a secular government institution.

Additionally, Catholic schools have always held as a fundamental right the necessity of educating young Catholics in the faith. If Green educational policies were enacted, schools would see an increase in non-Catholic populations with the resultant weakening of Catholic ethos and identity.

Green educational policies represent an assault upon the rights of Catholic parents to send their children to an educational institution of their choice. The funding discrimination proposed by the Greens would impact on hard-working parents and schools that manage their resources prudently.

Marriage: Catholic and Green

In Catholic teaching, God disposed man and women for each other so that they might be "no longer two but one" (Matthew 19:6). As the Catechism states: "In this way they are to live in love, be fruitful, and thus become a sign of God himself who is nothing but overflowing love" (*Catechism of the Catholic Church*, 1601-1605). Marriage for Catholics has always contained a sacramental element, that is, marriage is not only a contractual arrangement, given in free consent, affirmed as a lifelong union, with an openness to children, but also an act which is accepted and confirmed by God.

At this point in Australian life, when around half of marriages end in divorce, Catholic marriage takes on an added importance. When so much in life is relative, non-binding and can be overturned or revoked comparatively easily, (including Australia's no fault divorce) the absolute nature of Catholic marriage points to fidelity at the heart of God's nature and love for humanity.

Of course, not all Australians who undertake marriage may attribute this depth of commitment and fidelity to a marriage relationship. Increasingly marriage conducted by civil celebrants makes no mention of lifelong fidelity, nor of a commitment to children, nor of their indissolubility. Typical vows during such marriage ceremonies go no further than promises to comfort, honour, respect and share hopes and dreams.

The Australian Greens party is fundamentally indifferent to the nature of marriage itself, nor is it interested in the level of commitment or otherwise which couples may undertake. Its underlying view is to place marriage within a series of available "rights" open to all. Importantly marriage rights are placed within a greater series of rights concerning adoption, fostering, gender change and assisted reproductive treatment.

The Greens party does not have a marriage policy as such but a sex, sexuality and gender identity policy. This policy emphasises:

(1) Freedom of sex, sexuality and gender identity are fundamental human rights.
(2) Acceptance and celebration of diversity are essential for genuine social justice and equality.
(3) People have a right to their self-identified gender which is integral to people's lived experience as citizens and members of the community.
(4) Discrimination and vilification on the basis of sex, sexuality and gender identity is a significant cause of psychological distress, mental illness, and suicide.
(5) The health needs of all Australians should be provided for without discrimination of any kind; everyone has the right to have their specific health needs met with equality and respect.
(6) Society should be free of harassment, abuse, vilification, stigmatisation, discrimination, disadvantage or exploitation on the basis of the actual or assumed sex, sexuality or gender identity of a person or someone they are associated with.

In light of these principles, the Greens now outline a number of concrete aims in which marriage is to be understood:

(1) The legalisation of marriage between two consenting adults regardless of sex, sexuality or gender identity.
(2) All de facto relationships to have equal status in law and government policy regardless of sex, sexuality and gender identity.

(3) Equal access regardless of sex, sexuality and gender identity and marital status, to adopt and fostering, and assisted reproductive treatment.

Undoubtedly, the Greens party has no awareness of the purposes of marriage in relation to its lifelong nature, its centrality for the care and nurture of children, nor of the wider value it offers to society. Marriage which is promoted exclusively within a "rights driven" framework has removed any deeper understanding of the nature of marriage. For the Church marriage is the foundation on which communities are built, the underpinning first principle on which Western society rests. Without the formation of families based on lifelong fidelity and trust, with an emphasis on the greater good of the whole, it is impossible to expect society to also act in a corresponding manner. Placing marriage within a sex, sexuality and gender framework has altered its fundamental nature by placing the interests and desires of the individual above those of the whole.

The UK sociologist Dr Patricia Morgan has called attention to some of the cultural, social and economic changes that have occurred in Western nations.

Dr Morgan presented her paper, "What happens to marriage and families when the law recognises same sex marriage", to the House of Commons in March 2013. Of particular note, Dr Morgan pointed out that same sex marriage had weakened the connection between marriage and parenthood: "This was the principal factor that caused the collapse in marriage rates between heterosexuals in countries where gay marriage has been introduced as well as a sharp rise in cohabitation and the numbers of children born out of wedlock." Dr Morgan noted that she found no evidence to support assertions that gay marriage would bolster the institution.

Dr Morgan's work contained detailed analysis of marriage trends in Sweden, Norway, Denmark, Spain, Belgium, Canada and some American states where gay marriage had been legalised.

Dr Morgan also noted: "Same sex marriage is both an effect and a cause of the evisceration of marriage, especially the separation between this and parenthood." Importantly, for the Catholic church and its own critical role in the developing and upholding of the family, Dr Morgan explained that "gay marriage became conceivable only in those countries where marriage was already in crisis because of soaring out of wedlock births and cohabitation rates and invariably made such problems worse".

It is a common argument from pro-gay marriage advocates to suggest that widening the numbers of those who can participate in marriage will strengthen its overall status. Dr Morgan's research, particularly that focused on Spain (a country with same sex marriage since 2005), found that marriage actually decreased by around 15,000 per year for the first three years (2005-2007), but that since 2008 the decrease has doubled to 34,000 marriages less per year!

On a personal note (without any corroboration through research) Dr Morgan suggested that institutions which opposed the redefinition of marriage were likely to suffer some stigmatism for alleged lack of compassion and equal rights.

There is now significant evidence that this is occurring in those places which have redefined marriage. In Massachusetts, following same sex marriage laws, Catholic charities of Boston were forced to discontinue their adoption services rather than act against their religious principles by placing children with same sex couples. There is now a strong case to suggest that sexual rights take precedence over religious freedoms in the American context.

Massachusetts has now legislated to allow the teaching of homosexual and gender issues in schools and kindergartens, and denied parents who continuously object the right to withdraw their children from these classes.

Legislative actions against dissenting individuals have taken on an absurd and frivolous character. In New Mexico, the Supreme Court has ruled that the first amendment does not protect a photographer's right to decline to take pictures of a same sex commitment ceremony and in the United Kingdom the Christian owners of a bed and breakfast were fined for discrimination when they refused a gay couple a double-bed room.

While it is easy for me to suggest that such instances are amusing irritants caused by unthinking authorities, this is certainly not the experience of those who are forced to compromise or abandon deeply held religious beliefs that go to the heart of their faith and life. The Catholic Church should be neither indulgent nor gullible in the recognition of the advent of campaigns against its faith and teachings.

Catholicism has throughout its history understood itself as the primary organisation whereby a culture of life is presented to the wider world (regardless of customs or ethnic background). This Catholic understanding of life regards all stages of human existence from conception through to natural death as sacred. As such, Catholics oppose practices destructive of human life, including abortion, euthanasia, contraception, capital punishment, and the eradication of embryonic stem cells. In 1995 Pope John Paul II noted in *Evangelium Vitae*:

> ... man is called to a fullness of life which far exceeds the dimensions of this earthly existence, because it consists of sharing the very life of God. The loftiness of this supernatural vocation reveals the greatness and inestimable value of human life even in its temporal phase (2).
>
> Today, this proclamation is especially timely because of the extraordinary increase and gravity of threats to the life of individuals and peoples, especially where life is weak and defenceless (3).
>
> Unfortunately, this disturbing state of affairs, far from

decreasing, is expanding: with the new prospects opened up by scientific and technological progress there arise new forms of attacks on the dignity of the human being. At the same time a new cultural climate is developing and taking hold, which gives crimes against life a new and – if possible – even more sinister character, giving rise to further grave concern. Broad sectors of public opinion justify certain crimes against life in the name of the rights of individual freedom, and on this basis, they claim not only exemption from punishment but even authorisation by the State, so that these things can be done with total freedom and indeed with the free assistance of health care systems (4).

Today, there exists a great multitude of weak and defenceless human beings, unborn children in particular, whose fundamental right to life is being trampled on (5).

This view of freedom leads to serious distortions of life in society. If the promotion of the self is understood in terms of absolute autonomy, people inevitably reach the point of rejecting one another ... At this point, everything is negotiable, everything is open to bargaining, even the first of the fundamental rights, the right to life ... To claim the right to abortion, infanticide and euthanasia, and to recognise that right in law, means to attribute to human freedom a perverse and evil significance, that of absolute power over others and against others (20).

Pope John Paul II has forcefully critiqued much of what now occurs in Australia, and clearly exposed the corrupted moral thinking that has widely infiltrated our culture and society. In many ways, the Greens posturing on issues such as abortion and the various abortion pills (non-surgical abortion which uses mifepristone (RU486) and misoprostal) mirrors the view of an increasing number of Australians, particularly under 35 years of age.

Nevertheless although current majority thinking and the legislature continue to support a mainstream view Australian Catholics must continue to oppose such words and actions which continue to deny life to humanity's most vulnerable.

10

CATHOLICISM AND AUSTRALIAN CULTURE

Bogans: A permanent Australian underclass

The egalitarian nature of post-World War II Australia began to change significantly in the late 1970s, with the recognisable emergence of a substantial number of Australians markedly disengaged from the mainstream of Australian life and cultural aspirations. This phenomenon had been recognisable in other Western nations from an earlier period, particularly in the United Kingdom, yet Australians who were familiar with the wider world generally prided themselves on a presumption that such a state of affairs could not evolve here. Certainly, poor, undereducated and disadvantaged Australians have always existed and at times in our history have suffered disproportionately (as the 1920s and 1930s). Nevertheless, this was usually felt to be a temporary phenomenon and one in which hard work and persistence would enable individuals of determination to improve their lives and contribute strongly to the wider society.

However, a new and permanent phenomenon has arisen in Australia, which sees many people demotivated, disengaged from society, hostile towards our institutions and without a vision for life that might include material improvement, education, a cultural dimension or a notion of being loved by something beyond themselves. Indeed, this experience of life is permanently marred by lack of love, distrust, inability to form relationships, ineffectiveness in holding work, drug taking and powerlessness to engage with society on any level other than via antipathy and resentment. This new underclass appears to be growing substantially while remaining impervious to education or work related solutions.

Traditionally, Catholicism in its Australian context has orientated itself towards the poor, perhaps because of its Irish working class origins, a core constituency that would later be joined by other Catholic adherents from nations emerging from war and disruption. (Italians post-World War II and Vietnamese post 1974). This "poor" migration experience found natural support in a church which did not find itself as central to the establishment or workings of the nation, either in its colonial phase nor in the early post-federation decades. In this sense most of Australia's early Catholics were bound together naturally not only by religious affiliation but by economic similarity. Without doubt, the Church helped to form a common identity but also went much further than an organisation of purely religious devotion. Working men's groups, women's associations, young Catholic support groups of various forms all flourished in a community that saw itself as linked together across all of life's activities and endeavoured to provide cradle to grave care and identity.

This was a setting in which each Catholic parish had a youth group (Young Christian Workers) student groups (Young Christian Students) coupled with teams catering for different sports, at different times of the year. Parish dances, picnics, choirs, youth activities as well as participation in the life of the local Catholic schools gave parishes a natural centrality in the life of most Catholics. Regrettably, almost all of this has evaporated over the last 30 years and few parishes now offer much beyond a diminishing number of Mass times. The consequence of this new environment is that few parishioners know each other, or the priest, and engagement with the parish beyond Mass attendance is infrequent.

Paradoxically, the advent of this permanent Australian underclass was concurrent with the slow collapse of Catholic identity and the loss of energy required to sustain many of the activities taken for granted within Catholic parish life. I am not suggesting that there is any perceptible connection between these two developments, except to note that this offers significant opportunities for regrowth to Australian Catholic parishes particularly in the provision of pre-employment programs, work programs, youth development and cultural initiatives. This is a model of the Catholic parish which again offers to local people (of all backgrounds) a vision of care and connectedness across a more sizable dimension of human activity than is currently recognisable.

Australian businesses have in recent decades consistently complained about the high number of Australian born school leavers without basic skills in English and maths but also significantly without adequate presentation skills, understandings of democracy, or their own cultural backgrounds.

The deficiency of cultural insight has in some instances created a disregard and detachment from the culture of their native Australia. It is of little surprise that students who cannot articulate the significance of Shakespeare, Bradman, Murdoch, Hitler, Stalin or Thatcher, who are ignorant of World War II, the Anzac tradition or any Australian prime minister will be callous and cool towards their own society.

In many cases, Australian culture is little more than the latest entertainment show, a passing singer, or the most recent drunken footballer or texting cricketer! The effect of education that cannot delve below the surface is witnessed in the constant boredom and apathy displayed by most of these disengaged youth. From the Catholic perspective a life devoid of intellectual perspective is not only lacking in cultural depth but also the ability to consider life's significant religious questions. (faith, life, death, beauty and truth).

Underlying this cultural, educational and religious deficit is a lurking attitude of victimhood. Increasingly this group of Australians sees themselves as being failed or let down by government, teachers, or the "system". Nowhere is the idea prevalent that individual responsibility or determination plays any part in self-improvement, or the acquisition or maintenance of a job. Unfortunately, many of our institutions, which sometimes includes the Church, have encouraged this absolution from personal responsibility. An attachment to the status of "victim" allows the individual continual freedom in blaming "others". The consequence of such a view is to see no value in education or training, a passivity that will attempt nothing that requires effort, and an easy excuse for maintaining the status quo. All of this fosters continual misery, a strong narcissistic streak and an ongoing disconnection from Australian society.

From 2005-2012 I worked extensively with Sudanese refugees settled in Melbourne's northern suburbs. This group of people had undergone extensive persecution in Sudan for their Christian faith. Having been compelled to move countries they again endured harsh treatment in refugee settlements in various African countries, prior to commencing a new life in Australia. This young community (most parents were in their early 40s) had successfully spent a great deal of effort in maintaining their attachment to family values, faith precepts, and a psychology that suggested things would ultimately get better. This attachment was maintained over a ten year period in extremely harsh economic and political circumstances.

Naturally, arriving in an affluent Western nation would present another set of problems associated with cultural, linguistic and gender roles, given the generally patriarchal nature of the Sudanese family. Nevertheless, no one could have foreseen that it was actually exposure to and ultimately integration with Australia's underclass that would unravel this community.

The earliest casualty was the status and credibility of the Sudanese father, within the new host country. Most of these young fathers were ill-equipped for work in modern Australia and were almost entirely unable to move beyond Centrelink payments. For men who had previously supported their families and derived status from such a role to be replaced by "government" as the chief provider of the family was a deeply shocking and soul-destroying experience. Nevertheless, the biggest impact was not on the fathers themselves but on their teenage sons.

It was not long before teenage Sudanese boys, started to view their fathers as failures, unsuccessful in the "new world" and therefore not able to act as mentors, teachers and exemplars. This situation was heavily influenced by the environments and suburbs in which the Sudanese were placed. Effectively they entered a world in which "local Aussie fathers" were also missing or fully entrenched in their own "victimhood" mentality. It is not surprising that the rise of Sudanese gangs paralleled the local born versions.

I have lost count of the number of seminars I attended on the issues of Sudanese integration to be constantly told that finding work for Sudanese men was not a priority. Instead, the prime concern was that discrimination against the mothers and perpetuated gender sterotypes were no longer relevant in modern Australia. Almost exclusively programs for Sudanese integration, which focused on the skilling of women, alienated the men, and most seriously eroded their status. A viewpoint advanced by myself. (who worked with the community every day) that male employment was the key to Sudanese integration was downplayed, ignored or viewed as religious conservatism from the 1950s. My judgement that Sudanese integration will not be possible until this key issue is addressed is unfortunately confirmed each day as problems within this community remain unsolved, crime rates increase and gang style behaviour has become entrenched

The disconnect between the Sudanese community and mainstream Australians is best illustrated by the attitude of young Sudanese with whom I regularly engaged. I stood as character reference for one young lad of nineteen constantly involved in drug offences. This lad was fundamentally good yet was never offered any worthwhile training or employment, had made no worthwhile connections with locals and recognised early that financial strength and status could be achieved through drug dealing. The police for him were not to be taken seriously as he noted "all they did was talk". This lad wanted to change yet our dealings with him, from his perspective "offered nothing but taking money like my father and no longer having a life". This lad was murdered six months later, killed after an argument over a girl in which he received a screwdriver in the head. Ironically, he was left stricken in a driveway for over 30 minutes. No Sudanese young person thought to call police or ambulance, although many talked to him, offered him water and other assistance. When an ambulance was finally called by non-Sudanese neighbours, he died on arrival. The hospital verdict that early intervention would certainly have saved his life just added further pain. There will continue to be ongoing difficulties with this community as it deepens its fundamental belief that Australian institutions, police, ambulance services and Centrelink are to be avoided. The Sudanese community in some parts of Australia has learnt this from those amongst whom they live.

In my view, society has no possibility of replacing the family as the essential structure that inculcates values of respect, hard work and self-reliance. Most importantly, it is the family that usually orientates "free-will" into a positive force.

Modern Australia is now a nation of excuses, with most crime or failure to achieve conditioned by responses such as "I have no father", "my boyfriend left me", "I fell in with the wrong crowd", or "everybody else does it". At the heart of our society lies a destructive self-indulgence which gives us an excuse for doing what we want, every time, and blaming outside forces like schools, police or absent parents. Without the structure of family life, regulation by parents, including actively engaged fathers, and focusing young Australians on a life beyond themselves, we will find more young people morally vacuous in a society that highlights endless freedom but lacks the courage to speak of responsibility.

If there is one area of Australian life that symbolises our extensive freedom more than any other, it is the liberation of sex.

It was claimed that the removal of guilt, shame, anxiety or frustration around sexual issues would produce a society in which greater harmony, tolerance and respect between the sexes would flourish. After forty years of sexual liberation, however, it is hard to see a great deal of concrete evidence that "free will" within the sexual domain has produced liberation of any sort.

Divorce rates are the highest in our history, and failure rates for second marriages are over 80 per cent. Plainly, the custom and practice of marriage is under great stress. Indeed, this stress is regularly offered as a reason many couples delay such commitment or refuse to consider it at all. The cornerstone of relations between the sexes appears near collapse in many Australian communities, and particularly amongst those from undereducated or unemployed cohorts.

This group is noted for the formation of "families" in which no child has the same biological father, children have no ongoing relationship with their fathers, or where the man currently engaged in the role of "dad" is not the biological father of any of up to three, four or more children.

Relationships for many Australians are only of fleeting duration and often end in violent confrontation as quickly as they commenced. The dramatic upsurge in violence towards women and children is commonly associated with the rashness of such relationships, driven by an emotional childishness which imagines that liaisons with unstable and self-centred men will somehow result in happier outcomes, if tried over and over again.

Australian society has placed an emphasis and importance on sex which has actually increased violence towards women and children and greatly extended suspicion and apprehension between the sexes. For a growing number of Australian men lacking any real success in life and with non-existent employment prospects, the control of a woman is a last resort. Regrettably, it is usually the case that devotion and fidelity to a partnership is seen by many men as an action only required of the female. This attitude further erodes trust and extends violence. The tendency to change partners does nothing to actually change anything.

I have long since ceased to expect that this relationship chaos would result in a sense of shame or desire for privacy. In reality, the opposite is the case. These dramatic relationships produce scenes of great passion and foul language, often played out in public. The number of vigorous discussions I have heard on Melbourne trams, that focus on the size of male genitalia, or prowess in bed, or the requirement of a female partner to undergo breast surgery, are legion.

Today we have wholeheartedly linked human happiness with sexual activity and fulfilment. Unsurprisingly, sex has proved to be a disappointment to a great many. Yet, how could it be otherwise when we have removed its essential meaning and significance, namely its connection to love, grace and fidelity.

Like much also in our society, the consequences of total sexual freedom are not only suffered by the individuals concerned but by children as well.

Modern Australian children experience a highly sexualised world from a young age. Our television, movies and radio, along with the fashion industry, all seem to reward exhibitionist behaviour from the mid-primary years. The examples of young female music performers, boy bands and the like usually ensure that sex is also at the forefront of the mind of teenage Aussies.

Childhood years seem eroded earlier and earlier with many Australian children overindulged with the latest technology, games and fashions but concurrently enduring acute loneliness and disconnection from parents and the wider family. Within lower socio-economic groups these guiding influences are mostly absent throughout a young person's life. It is not hard to see this downgrading of childhood as the prelude to the bored, disinterested individual voluntarily imprisoned in rooms, where internet games and online friends become more central than reality. The possibility of change, in which such a life might be transformed into an engaged, interested and contributing member of society, has entirely evaporated by that individual's mid-twenties. Without the support of family, employment and structure of friends, a culture of victimhood is set to repeat itself through another generation.

Australian society is producing too many people who are happy to highlight any number of events that can be twisted into a narrative of continual victimhood. This worldview not only destroys individual initiative, drive and vision, it also robs those who exhibit it of a genuine future. Our society has a significant stake in eradicating its development, its nurture, and its passing onto younger Australians.

There is no significant institution in Australian life, apart from the Catholic Church, which can make any sizeable inroads into this problem in the short term. Parliament, police and schools have all in different ways failed to make an impression. At its heart this is a spiritual issue and is one where Catholicism has significant insights. The support of marriage, family stability for children and the value of community are all positive Catholic values and ones which fundamentally challenge the prevailing worldview.

Nevertheless, few parishes or priests are skilled or equipped to present this ethos unless a change in the Church's priorities can be wrought. This requires parishes, already implanted in most suburbs, to again engage with their communities, particularly those not currently worshipping within their walls. The resources of parishioners, the physical buildings, the partnership with schools, all allow endless possibilities for supporting those who are disengaged. Work programs, youth groups, mentoring opportunities, relationship support and training are all areas that have diminished in recent government funding and generally do not exist on a local level. This provides a significant opportunity for the Church to nurture and strengthen society as well as fulfilling its tasks as set down by Christ. The provision of welfare is valuable but it is not enough; changing values, lives and creating opportunity is the business of the Church. Recent changes have seen a retreat into a smaller and narrower world. This needs to change, not only on the part of the Church but also across the nation as a whole.

Further Reading

Umberto Eco, *On Ugliness*, Rizzoli, New York, 2011.

11

Free Will: Chaos or Control?

The *Catechism of the Catholic Church* describes the dignity of the human person as enveloped and embraced by the gift of human freedom;

> God willed that man should be left in the hand of his own council, so that he might of his own accord seek his creator and freely attain his full and blessed perfection by cleaving to him. Man is rational and therefore like God, he is created with free will and is master over his acts.

The *Catechism* further states:

> Freedom is the power, rooted in reason and will, to act or not to act, to do this or that, and so to perform deliberate actions on one's own responsibility. By free will one shapes one's own life. Human freedom is a force for growth and maturity in truth and goodness; it attains its perfection when directed towards God (1730-1731).

Nowhere is this full understanding of free will less acknowledged than in modern Australian communal life. The conviction that free will is a governing principle of human life has largely disappeared from educational institutions, the justice system, political theory and indeed communal living. Australians now broadly believe themselves to be in the thrall of forces or internal drives largely beyond their control and for which they can undertake no effective measures of resistance or change. Various forms of neo-paganism have entered into the Australian psyche which sees individuals as wedged between differing dualistic forces, surrounded by a nature-based cosmology or in need of attachment with feminine spiritual forces to balance destructive male divine principles (usually found in Christian expression). The end result of this is a disregard for rational explanation and greater reliance on interpretations realised through fate, luck or emotions.

This can be manifest in a number of differing ways but often conforms to thinking in which all institutions are constantly in need of "reform". Regularly this "reform" takes on a life of its own and idealises aggressive change around issues not even thought of in the recent past. This " reform-change" model, followed by more "reform-change" has resulted in very unstable political governance in recent years, but more deeply reflects an inability to think rationally and deeply over issues, and particularly to fail to foresee the reasonably predictable outcomes of actions.

This thinking is also prevalent in some of the social issues we face, particularly around those that are superficially thought to affect no-one but the individuals concerned and promoted as issues in which human rights are centrally implicated.

A major challenge we currently face concerns illegal drug usage, especially among young Australians, which has involved a sharp increase in methamphetamine and ecstasy usage. Methamphetamine increases the volume of dopamine in the brain, a neurotransmitter associated with the experience of pleasure which produces sensations of euphoria, but can easily lead to addiction.

At no stage in Australian history have we been faced with the perfect storm of vast arrays of cheap illegal drugs and a generation of Australians under 35 years of age so dedicated to their rights in pursuit of private pleasures. Instinctively, it has not been long before calls for drug legislation and drug decriminalisation have emerged.

Such calls usually highlight the failure of current deterrence polices, the increase in government revenue to be gained from taxing drugs, the right of Australians to live their lives free of government intervention, and an alleged reduction in crime that would emerge post-liberalisation. Underlying all of this is a philosophical stance that claims a freedom for individuals to do whatever they please, provided they do not directly harm others. This viewpoint is a fanatical form of individualism which tolerates no government or societal input into moral questions.

The Church cannot remain silent in the face of this situation. Catholics have always understood that the benefits of community living revolve around a series of rights and responsibilities that have far more substance than any notions of non-inference with others. Catholics value freedom but not without order, for it is order that conditions our rights. Within a Catholic-moral perspective, it is occasionally appropriate to sacrifice freedom for order, and also appropriate to sometimes downplay order for freedom, yet the two are never disconnected, or one emphasised to the exclusion of the other.

For the Church, freedom is of the utmost importance yet it is not just the freedom to satiate our own personal desires to the exclusion of our neighbours. Christ's teaching to "do unto others as you would have them do to you" (Matt 7:12) has not been abrogated in Catholic thinking. Indeed for Catholics, the freest individuals are not those who adhere only to their own desires, but rather those who understand freedom within the context of service to others.

Here, the practice of regular drug-taking actually reduces the freedom of individuals, as it totally limits the range of those individuals' interests. Indeed, those people usually lose spouses, friends, interests, hobbies, sports and employment as they pursue an increasingly narrow world in which drugs become the single and most important attraction.

Within Catholic theology, such a situation means self-centred parasitical lives without the fullness of God's love, impaired relationships and broken families. Drug addicts are fundamentally bored with life, have no concept of real contentment and lack the ability to see beyond the immediate. Such enslavement is really the embodiment of hell.

Our society is at risk of progressively making no demands on our citizens in terms of responsibility. Certainly we have more laws, statutes and regulations governing our behaviour, yet these are prohibitions that do not primarily require or teach responsibility to ourselves or others.

Despite endless new laws pertaining to dogs, pollution, noise, speech, car parking, no games in parks or the illegality of changing light bulbs without proper registration, concurrently we are at risk of witnessing self-indulgence and radical personal freedom as becoming our highest good.

The argument that current laws surrounding illegal drugs increase criminality, encourage corruption and pervert law enforcement are at best only partially true. Certainly illegality has its attractions to some young people and others with underdeveloped reasoning powers, yet primarily the costs of drug-taking are born by society (in the support that must be provided for recovery) by spouses, by children and by the individual concerned. The creation of more non-functioning Australians, with poor opportunities for recovery or reform is not a burden we can actually afford. Advocates of drug liberalisation may suggest our jails are currently full of fundamentally good people driven to crime through addiction, but does anyone really imagine that numbers of non-functioning addicts would actually reduce because of decriminalisation? It is much more likely that numbers would dramatically increase.

It is often suggested that we are not "winning the war on drugs".

This may well be true, but nor are we winning the war against death and no one suggests we should abandon cancer research, close hospitals or abolish medical schools on the grounds that these are all failing miserably.

Underlying Australia's drug problem is a new philosophical position which suggests that you have no right to tell me what to do, provided I harm nobody else.

In these circumstances, Catholic moral theology, which sees responsibility to God as central, is the only effective counterweight to this rampant narrow individualism. For Catholicism, freedom is not simply doing our own thing, but a call to right thinking, willing and acting.

Edmund Burke, the Irish philosopher and politician, noted the dangers for a society heading in Australia's direction: "But what is liberty without wisdom, and without virtue? It is the greatest of all possible evils; for it is folly, vice and madness, without tuition or restraint."

Our society currently exhibits an expanding sense of complaint, disorder and self-indulgence. This is manifest in our public drunkenness and increased drug usage, and in the dramatic decline in our community values. Significant numbers of Australians are no longer prepared to commit to moral stances but increasingly happy to describe themselves as "non-judgemental". The reality of this position ultimately leads to a lack of care for individuals and a significant disregard for wider society.

Catholicism must find ways again to promote its alternative, profound understanding of the value of humanity and the actions required to initiate change. A deeper awareness among Catholics of their Church's fundamental opposition to the above attitudes and necessary counter-cultural role is a good place to start.

12

CATHOLICISM AND GOVERNMENT

Australian society currently seems increasingly indifferent to issues of freedom, morality and religion. Ironically in recent years we have been subjected to the fastest expansion of Commonwealth legislation in our history, many laws being concerned with freedom and religious issues. Chris Berg of the Institute of Public Affairs noted that in 2010 another 6,369 pages of law had been added, spread over a staggering 150 new acts of parliament. Berg rightly suggests that, rather than living in an era of greater freedom and deregulation, in reality our government is expanding its intervention into more areas of our economic and community life.

Berg observes two aspects of this legislative expansion that Australians are unlikely to have considered:

> Firstly, the more laws a government passes, the busier it is. We have increasingly busy governments. Australia's legal and regulatory system is being continuously shuffled around. Continuous change has its consequences. To take one of the more prominent examples, in the last few years businesses have had to get up to speed with the niceties of Workplace Agreements, then the complexities of Work Choices, and now the nuances of Fair Work.
>
> Secondly, the regulatory framework which governs the economy is increasingly complex. Longer laws are more

complex laws. The *Work Choices Act* was 762 pages. The *Fair Work Act* was 651. People (not just lawyers) have to read and understand the terms (Micromanagement in the Regulatory State, the Drum unleashed, Chris Berg 25 January 2011).

Condemning the volume and complexity of Commonwealth Law, Chief Justice Patrick Keane of the Federal Court observed, "Opening the *Tax Act* is like entering the door to a parallel universe".

This trend should serve as a potent warning to Australian Catholics, as such legislative inclinations throughout the world have never led to greater freedom for overseas Catholics. In 2012, the Australian Human Rights Commission met with considerable opposition from concerned Australians as it sought to extend its Human Rights and Anti-Discrimination Bill 2012.

Simon Breheny, director of the Legal Rights Project at the free market think tank, the IPA, suggested:

> The Australian Human Rights Commission does not defend fundamental rights such as the right to free speech and property. Instead it selectively defends a human rights agenda determined entirely by the left. ... By supporting the draft Human Rights and Anti-discrimination Bill 2012, the Australian Human Rights Commission has demonstrated hostility to freedom of speech, freedom of association and freedom of Religion (IPA media release on Human rights Commission).

A number of examples from the draft legislation had the potential to impact on the Catholic Church:

- Broadening the definition of discrimination to include conduct that "offends and insults" (Clause 19.2).
- Making it easier for a person to claim they were discriminated against, by requiring them to establish only that they were personally offended, not that a reasonable person would have been offended (Clause 19.2).

- Reducing the legal protection of a person accused of discrimination, by declaring them guilty unless they prove their innocence, ie the onus of proof is reversed (Clause 124.1).
- Restricting the right to legal representation (Clause 110.4).
- Requiring them to pay all the costs of their own defence even if they are found to be innocent (Clause 133).

Had this draft legislation successfully passed through parliament the potential to cause offence to others would have been severely expanded. The impact on freedom of religion would have made it an offence (with potential for judicial consequences), of simple acts like wearing a crucifix in public (where another person might be offended or claim to be offended because of religion).

The Draft legislation would also make any debate about religious beliefs or practices unlawful if others were to be offended by such debate, due to their own particular faith.

While this legislative initiative has not become law, without the vigilance of free speech advocates, it may well have done so. Paradoxically, the Church did not engage in any coordinated campaign against this potentially restrictive legislation. Nevertheless, this initiative underlined the readiness of some sections of our polity to seek greater control over areas of Australian life, previously thought to be beyond government involvement.

This tendency of governments to increase controls over the lives of citizens is often fostered by the unthinking calls by many Australians for greater government intervention when some situation appears unsatisfactory to some groups. These calls can be for additional road safety by-laws or council regulations in relation to a host of local problems, or for government intervention in moral or religious spheres. Prescribed educational works in American and European schools that promote alternative families seem to meet the criteria.

While in Australia we do not have such prescribed curricula, many organisations promote material and websites supporting "Rainbow Families" that are designed for children. Rainbow Families Victoria produces kits suitable for maternal child health centres, childcare centres, kindergartens and the early years of primary school. Darebin council has given financial support for the production of such material although I am unaware of any such material on "How Catholics Live" being promoted.

It may be a strained analogy, but this tendency to view government as the provider and enforcer of services, laws and morality has increased during a period of weakness in Australian Catholicism. Coupled with this inclination to view government as the new "divine" provider, a concurrent loss of individual responsibility encourages government intervention. Governments already intervene where parents are seen to be irresponsible in their handling of child support, finances, debts, school truancy or lack of parenting skills, but is it the role of governments to provide questionable moral education as well? The high Australian divorce rate, underage drinking and the increased use of drugs, all provide ample evidence of the inability of government to encourage moral responsibility.

Instead of this unbridled extension of new laws, Catholics should focus on rebuilding Australia's moral consensus. This is a long and difficult task, yet no other institution is capable of such an endeavour, given the negligible size or influence of other religious groups.

The family, which remains the key vehicle for the transmission of values to children, is struggling to carry out this essential role. Here the Church could provide greater services to families through courses, family orientated ministries and greater targeted support. Single women who make the courageous decision not to abort their children also need stronger support.

The Church might consider the development of an independent

Catholic think-tank to begin the process of considering the Church's response to these issues and also begin discussion and promotion of ideas which remain unaired. Such an organisation might consider questions regarding the increased size of both federal and state governments as well as the impact of governance issues on the freedom of Catholics to fully live and develop their faith.

Concerns over increasing state interference in the freedom of ordinary citizens are not new. British Prime Minister Margaret Thatcher (1979-1991) drew attention to aspects of the "nanny state in the 1980s and Pope John Paul II placed the Catholic concept of the person within the vision of an an unimpeding society:

> According to *Rerum Novarum* and the whole social doctrine of the Church, the social nature of man is not completely fulfilled by the state, but is realised in various intermediary groups, beginning with the family and including economic, social, political and cultural groups which stem from human nature itself, and have their own autonomy, always with a view to the common good (*Centesimus Annus*, 13).

Again in *Centesimus Annus*, John Paul reflected on recent developments in Western nations:

> In recent years the range of such intervention has vastly expanded, to the point of creating a new type of state, the so-called "Welfare State". This happened in some countries in order to respond better to many needs and demands, by remedying forms of poverty and deprivation unworthy of the human person. However, excesses and abuses, especially in recent years, have provoked very harsh criticisms of the Welfare State, dubbed the "Social Assistance State". Malfunctions and defects in the Social Assistance State are the result of an inadequate understanding of the tasks proper to the State. There again, the principle of subsidiarity must be respected, a community of a higher order should

not interfere in the internal life of a community of a lower order, depriving the latter of its functions, but rather should support in a case of need and help to coordinate its activity within the activities of the rest of society, always with a view to the common good (*Centesimus Annus*, 48).

Individuals who have come to expect governments to support the entirety of their lives are essentially downgrading their own fullness of humanity. A robust nation is based on individual responsibility, a vibrant Catholic religious expression and a strong notion of democratic subsidiarity.

The present condition of the European Union should be a cause of concern for Australian Catholics. In recent years the gulf between the desires of the average citizen for increased democracy, lower taxes, and less regulation have seen many European Union nations vote for less integration and greater local independence. These results are often ignored by the largely unelected bureaucratic class. The resultant loss of trust has seen a substantial increase in both far-right (France) and far left (Greece) political parties.

Pope Benedict XVI has even suggested that the European Union cannot succeed without recognising its Catholic-Christian values. Benedict noted that the European Union did not suddenly create a set of shared values and insights after the 1960s:

> ... rather it is these shared values that have given birth to and were like a 'gravitational force' that drew the countries together and inspired them to form a union. When the Church recalls the Catholic roots of Europe, it is not seeking a special status for itself, instead, it is calling Europeans to remember that the values that brought peace to the continent and freedom and dignity to its people must be allowed to continue nourishing it (Catholic.news.com/0904655).

During Benedict's ad limina visit to the United Kingdom in February

2010 he called on the bishops of England, Scotland and Wales to contest recent government legislation which contained elements of "ideological equality". The Pope argued that "such legislation limits the freedom of religious communities to act in accordance with their beliefs and actually violates the natural law upon which the equality of all human beings is grounded". In this instance Pope Benedict sought to preserve religious freedom through an appeal to the reason and truth of natural law.

The introduction of such "equality" laws does mean that Catholic adoption agencies, by refusing to allow homosexual couples to adopt, will be forced to shut down, or act against their conscience. Rightly, Benedict's concern is to challenge "radical ideological" equality and return consideration of equality to questions of truth, common sense and biological realities.

The advent of these radical legislative measures in the European Union and the United States of America point to the beginnings of a new form of challenge and discrimination against Catholicism. Australian Catholics should not expect to remain immune from their advances.

Further Reading

Anthony Fisher, *Catholic Bioethics for a New Millennium*, Cambridge University Press, 2011.

13

A Confident Catholic Future

The prevailing condition of Australian Catholicism is not terminal nor untreatable, but it is under considerable stress.

Clearly, it is possible to articulate substantial reasons and credible evidence as to why the Church seem to be in decline, particularly in comparison to past generations.

Mass attendance has lessened although this can be rationalised by reference to busier lives, mobile populations, loss of authority, clergy abuse, an anti-Catholic media focus or a proliferation of secular and pagan philosophies challenging the Catholic centrality of the past, but lifestyle and convenience issues can never justify loss of faith.

This situation may even be comforting to some, who seem happy to adapt to the "new norm" of a smaller and allegedly more faithful Church. However this position is reckless and risks subjecting the Church to permanent disappearance from the lives of most Australians.

The Church as revealed by Christ and accepted by the first disciples was never intended to be a "remnant", smallish and faithful fraternity, concerned primarily with its own interests or survival. It was intended by Christ to be a vehicle for the salvation of the world, the conversion of all with its long standing missionary commitment to the Kingdom of God. I can see nothing but a complete and radical boldness in this proclamation. In the understanding of Jesus, the complete transformation of individuals, societies and culture was intended as the "new normal".

Certainly, Catholic history including the experience in Australia has always revealed a robust level of hostility to the Church. Nothing has changed. Nevertheless, this opposition is not the only issue. The more serious matter has been the accommodation of some Catholics with liberal Australian society and an adoption of a "rights agenda" which is actually anti-Catholic in expression.

The Church must quickly recognise this has not worked and now risks substantial harm.

A Catholicism that is not noticeably distinct from other Christians or its host culture is unlikely to attract or maintain a new generation searching for community, intellectual inquiry and faithfulness not available in secular Australia.

Public Space – Workplace

Across many sectors of Western society there has been an observable rise in anti-Catholic rhetoric and behaviour. This animus has now reached a stage where individual Catholics and the wider Church are noticing what is beginning to appear as a concerted disparagement and revulsion. While anti-Catholic attitudes and actions in Europe and the United States are on the rise we now see signs emerging that Australia is following a similar path.

In 2004, the Italian Catholic Rocco Buttiglione was nominated by his government for a term as Justice Commissioner of the European Union. His nomination was vigorously opposed by many sub-sections of the European community, exclusively because of his orthodox Catholic family values in regard to matters of homosexuality, marriage and the raising of children. Forced to withdraw his nomination Buttiglione insightfully noted the change that had taken place:

The new soft totalitarianism that is advancing on the left wants to have a State religion. It is an atheistic, nihilistic religion, but it is a religion that is obligatory for all ("What place for God in Europe?" *Christian Science Monitor*, February 2005).

In 2010, a conservative political candidate in the United Kingdom was quickly deselected for expressing concerns over homosexuality. The apparent political incompatibility of electoral success with what remains traditional Catholic teaching suggests individuals who hold these views will be increasingly unlikely to represent major political parties in the future. Concurrently with the difficulties of a political life for those holding orthodox Catholic values is the wider question of the space allowed the Church on moral questions on which it has always spoken publically.

In Australia, Church influence on debates about such issues as assisted dying and euthanasia is increasingly disregarded when such views are widely regarded as outdated and discriminatory. Curiously, the 2014 criticism surrounding the suspension of the medical licence for Dr Philip Nitschke (who is alleged to have assisted a man to commit suicide without recommending counselling) was not led by any Church, but by the secular organisation beyondblue (an anti-depression initiative) and its outspoken chairman Jeff Kennett. This media focus suggests that religious arguments will be increasingly replaced by those from the "secular caring" industry. However, beyondblue's position did not focus on opposition to euthanasia as such, but on breaches of process and responsibility for not referring the individual for further specialist treatment.

Catholicism must be prepared to take up a more assertive stance within the public square. There will always be significant numbers of Australians and media commentators who believe the Church should confine its public comments to doctrinal matters, yet the Church cannot adhere to such strictures. Catholicism is necessarily public, its institution (schools and hospitals) and concerns with relationships, wealth and the environment being public. Most importantly, Christ's ministry and redemptive actions are public. From the standpoint of believers and non-believers alike, Australian society would be significantly diminished if the Church is successfully disconnected from its public role.

The consequences of a diminished public role can be seen in the realities for many European and American Catholics. Catholic foster parents, teachers and medical practitioners (working in public institutions) have often found themselves suspended, disciplined and dismissed under various forms of "culture and diversity" codes. Banishing Catholicism from expressing its legitimate public concerns represents a form of persecution. How otherwise can we describe such a situation where one sector is circumscribed in such a manner?

Australian Catholicism needs to regain a passion for the public dimensions of the faith. Our connection with individual workplaces, with employer groups, with political groups, think-tanks and the vast array of community and sporting clubs must be strengthened. Catholicism has important community dimensions of faith, loyalty and humility to present to Australian life. (Here two promising initiatives include www.cwb.org and www.catholicsinbusiness.org).

This is an area undeniably as important as worship and parish life as the public dimensions of the faith are indisputably central to the Church's mission. Without these public dimensions the Church risks detachment from its host Australian culture. Such a rupture is incompatible with the centrality of Christ's call in the lives of each individual Australian.

Youth

World Youth Day has been one of the most successful initiatives of the Catholic Church over recent decades. Initiated by Pope John Paul

II in 1985, a series of World Youth Days has been held in differing nations across the world since then on a regular basis. Australia (Sydney) hosted World Youth Day in 2008 while the 1995 World Youth Day closing Mass in the Philippines set a world record for the largest number of people gathered for a single religious event (seven Million). Despite the international success of World Youth Day, the reality on the ground for most Australian Catholic parishes is discouraging. The cohort of 16 to 26-year-olds is largely missing from the life of the Church and despite some local success, most parishes seem unappealing to the young. Parishes that are side by side with their local primary school often appear to fare no better in engaging the young or their parents. The Australian Bishops Commission for Pastoral Life has devoted some excellent resources, training and national support focusing on youth ministry. There are a number of important goals that have been established by the Bishops Commission:

- Personal and spiritual growth begins in childhood and continues through the young adult years and beyond. This development does not happen in isolation, and youth ministry needs to be aware of the support and ministry with children, young adults and parents to enable a holistic approach.
- To draw young people into responsible participation in the life, mission and work of the Catholic faith community.
- To empower young people to live as disciples of Jesus Christ in our World today.

These goals are excellent, yet there remains in many parishes a practical disconnect between goals and realities. The fact remains that unless parishes initiate local enterprise and place this as the number one parish ambition, there will remain a lack of energy and enthusiasm for youth development.

Additionally, there remains a philosophical change that is a prerequisite for success with young people, namely that the Church must be seen as having something to offer that cannot be found elsewhere. This necessitates serious local consideration for what might be offered to prepare young people for the longer journey of faith within the Catholic community and commitment to the good of Australian society.

In the current political environment, youth unemployment is a key factor in the demotivation of many young Australians in pursuing their dreams, developing resilience and seeing themselves as valuable to their wider community.

This, in truth, is an aspect of the critical task given to all Catholics of finding and undertaking their God-given vocation. It is the understanding and discovery of individual vocation that drives service. Without an unfolding sense of vocation the young risk rushing from one project or dream to another, without completing anything of substance.

A Catholic youth focus on vocation represents a unique offering. Modern Australia offers nothing of this sort, indeed the opposite is true, as our society constantly tells young people to discover who they are, "to thine own self be true", don't let anyone tell you what to do, form your own identity and discover yourself before you can do anything.

Catholic youth work must highlight that "to thine own self be true" is actually found in the service of others.

It is therefore important that local Catholic youth activities have this service dimension. It is not just about us, or building up our young people, but allowing them to see in service, the fundamental joy that sustains a vibrant, relevant and faith-filled life.

The discovery of vocation is a unique Catholic approach which is radically counter-cultural and offers young Australians of all backgrounds an alternative to the modern self-indulgent focus on individuality alone (www.thecyaproject.org).

Western Civilisation and Culture

Western civilisation and culture is a broad concept that includes ethical values, social norms and political systems, along with artistic, philosophic, literary and legal dimensions. My contention is that despite the changing and evolving of these dimensions at the heart of its long standing heritage is the Catholic Church. Catholicism has been central to humanity's understanding of itself throughout Western history, in a way no other institution has managed to achieve. This key role remains today and can be witnessed clearly in the spiritual, political and humanistic leadership role in the papacy. Modern day popes maintain this leadership role not just in a European subset of humanity but throughout the world.

Certainly Catholicism now has a global dimension, but it speaks to the world out of concepts formed at its beginning and packaged as Western cultural notions. These include the freedom of the individual, the emancipation of women and the equality of racial groups. In this very practical way, Catholicism performs its Christ-given task to transform humanity.

> There is no longer Jew nor Greek, there is neither slave nor free, there is no male or female for you are all one in Christ Jesus (Galatians 3:28).
>
> For we were all baptised by one spirit, to form one body, whether Jew or Gentile, slave or free, we were all given one spirit to drink (I Corinthians 12:13).

This task finds its fulfilment in the great commission of Christ:

> All authority has been given to me in heaven and on earth. Go therefore and make disciples of all nations, baptising

them in the name of the Father and the Son and the Holy Spirit, teaching them to observe all that I command you, and lo, I am with you always to the end of the age (Matthew 28:18.20)

In recent years a disconnection between Catholicism and its vitalising role in Western culture has begun to appear. This disconnection has resulted in a paralysis within a culture that appears to no longer support or promote its fundamental values. Indeed, these values themselves appear no longer to be seen as central. The values which gave Western civilisation its vocation to the world are now encapsulated in a form that believes only in the right of individuals to do and live as they please. Western civilisation and culture have begun to serve themselves and no longer highlight the equality and liberation that lead to service for all. Additionally, it seems Western culture and thinking now seek to live without any meaningful understanding of their essential heartbeat as lived through Catholicism.

Unfortunately, I cannot foresee a thriving and viable Western civilisation if this move to disconnect the Western body of spirituality, culture and values from its heart is successful. In my view, we cannot speak of Western culture, in any meaningful way, without Catholicism. Consequently, it is a real concern that education at primary, secondary and tertiary levels, regarding the centrality of Western history and culture and the Church's animating role, are almost totally absent from our curricula, even in Catholic schools.

We cannot expect young Australians to understand and treasure our civilisation if we subconsciously disparage it by refusing to teach it. Further, it is not surprising that young Australians subsequently cannot see the importance of Catholicism when we fail to treasure the culture and civilisation it has created.

Rights, Pagans and Media

Australian society is progressively undergoing a transition away from its former adherence to Western cultural ideas and the centrality of Catholic thinking. What we are transitioning towards is less than clear. This movement can be seen most clearly in the language of rights. Philosophically the highest good in modern Australia is equality. This now transcends freedom, justice or commitments to the wider society. Central to this domination of "equal" thinking and behaviour is an understanding that judgements upon others cannot be made. Hence for many people, the murderer or rapist and their victims are all now equally victims; yet this tolerance does not extend to Christian religious views.

All judgements now depend on the circumstances or backgrounds of the various individuals and no easy value judgement can be made. Equality of victimhood has meant a weakening of the distinction between individuals and their actions, with the consequence that those who commit crimes may feel victims of their past, their families, or the system. In basing our fundamental decision-making only on issues of equality we have moved away from considerations of right or wrong and justice. With the weakening of Catholicism and the absence of God, individuals and their various circumstances are the only measure that counts.

Undoubtedly, rights language is philosophically based on strong perceptions that all people have the right to control their own lives and actions, providing no hurt comes to others. In Catholic terms this philosophy rejects notions of responsibility. For Catholics it is entirely appropriate to consider individual rights but such rights must be balanced with responsibilities and sacrifice to the needs of others, something that is currently overlooked in Australian society.

The pervasive nature of this "rights philosophy" can also be seen in other challenges to Catholicism.

Today, it is common to hear many people make a distinction between being "religious" and being "spiritual". This contrast usually suggests that the religious dimension inhabited by Catholicism is old, authoritarian and primarily concerned with behavioural rules. Spirituality, on the other hand is liberating, and focused on personal fulfilment and a search for "your truth". This philosophical distinction has seen many people "collect" different aspects of theology, meditation, yoga, etc, rolling them into a "personalised" brand of "faith" without connection to any traditional religious basis. Many highlight their "spirituality", based on their vegetarianism, their meditation and the number of yoga classes they attend.

This feature of modern Australian life has witnessed significant numbers of former Catholics leave the Church and adopt these personalised spiritualities often citing a failure of Catholicism to appeal to their "inner being".

While these "spiritualities" are highly subjective, usually offer no community life and make unfair statements about church life and teaching, their continual growth should now be a concern for all Catholics. A coordinated response to this situation needs consideration. Significantly, the rejection of the Church in this case is not on intellectual criteria, but on issues of "personalised spirituality". The recent deterioration of many Catholic orders, who used to provide spiritual direction and organised retreats, also needs reviewed consideration and action (www.renewalcentre.com).

The traditional media is undoubtedly under significant stress with the growth in online content severely affecting the future of free-to-air-television, newspapers, magazines and community news. The loss of advertising dollars means that for some of these media, recovery will be difficult in future years.

The Church in Australia needs to expand its online content, internet, television, radio and blogs in a major effort to connect with Australians who are using this new media in huge numbers. A coordinated policy in this area is essential. For many under forty, new media is the major source of news, views, political understandings sports and spirituality. To be absent from this media environment (as Catholicism currently is) amounts to a serious impairment of community engagement and contact.

An interesting case study concerns Venezuela. Using legislation, fines, advertising pressure and control of paper for printing, the government over the last decade has managed to politically control mainstream media. Forced to find alternatives to traditional news and political views, Venezuelans have turned significantly to online content. In June 2014 alone, there were ten million new visitors to particular websites. This situation should give great encouragement to the Church as to what can be done with a coordinated and determined approach that would see Catholics turn to websites and blogs that highlight normative teachings, spirituality and liturgy.

This new environment has the additional benefits of allowing Catholicism to control its own content and not be subject to the filters or prejudice sometimes exhibited by particular media outlets. I note with interest that all current AFL clubs control media through their own websites with traditional sports columnists generally using these avenues as reliable information sources.

These football clubs also seek to control the "experience" of the supporter, through club television, player interviews, dedicated programs, fundraising, charity and junior members. This environment allows clubs to talk directly to supporters, understand each club's philosophy and intentions, and to engage directly with club officials and other supporters. Failure to engage and communicate in this way will be taken increasingly as disregard for the thoughts, concerns and hopes of supporters. Here is a first-rate opportunity for the Church to interconnect in the lives of both practising and uncommitted Catholics, along with those seeking deeper meaning in life in commitment to Christ.

The Catholic Church needs to rebuild a "parallel universe" that places itself alongside the secular, agnostic, and self-orientated society which has now become common in Australia. This secular society will not be encouraged to open itself to alternative visions of Australia in future years. As the Church has effectively "paralleled" the school system, other areas of our corporate life must be safeguarded and preserved in like manner. Our parishes, media, young Catholics and working Catholics must find a level of support in these dimensions of life that is currently missing.

Needed more than ever are the beauty of the Church (in buildings and liturgy), the direction of Mary and the saints, practical teaching and guidance, social outreach and the fundamental core of service to others. For the sake of all Australians, Catholicism needs to be a revitalised, energised and resilient voice in modern life.

14

What's to Be Done?

Three achievable initiatives

In September 2010 Pope Benedict XVI established a pontifical council for promoting the "New Evangelisation". This new evangelisation was to be focused on "re-proposing" the Gospel, notably in regions where the roots of Christianity are deep, but to those who have experienced a serious crisis of faith caused by secularisation. The Church in Western nations should be at the forefront of renewed endeavours to connect with the two "generations" of Catholics (those aged 50-60 and 20-35) who have been lost to the Church. In both these "generations" an initial connection may have been established but has failed to develop beyond the early school years.

These "generations" have also grown and developed in societies which by their nature do not regard religious values as normative or as offering anything particularly unique or worthy of retention. Increasingly, within these age groups there is an all-pervasive attitude of indifference towards the Church.

Pope Benedict was right in highlighting this direct threat to Catholicism, now found in Western nations, and in acknowledging that a "business as usual" model cannot continue within our parishes and organisations if a severe diminishing of Catholic influence is to be averted.

An obvious difficulty arises. How do Catholic parishes share their faith with those who do not connect with a parish community and have given up any participation in the life of the Church?

A major thrust of this book is that Catholicism has stalled in its engagement with that wider community. If we are not found within workplaces, sporting clubs or constantly debating current issues of concern to others, then how can we expect serious engagement with us. The spiritual life of Western citizens is of utmost concern to the Catholic Church but it must be rooted in trust gained through engagement in the activities that people usually undertake: education, employment, sports clubs and family services. It is an incomplete picture, if in blaming the rise of secularisation and government intervention for the reduction of Catholic influence, we ourselves have further withdrawn from the activities where people are generally to be found.

Workplaces

The greatest gap in Catholic engagement with Western society is its lack of influence within workplaces. It is vitally important also that the Church move from inactive observer status to a position in which it has positive initiatives, programs, ideas and personnel. This will require a change in the way the Church works. It will require working within business, to understand its values and attitudes, and using a partnership model to develop a flexibility that can identify problems, connections and new ways forward.

Identifying gaps and niche areas of work is essential. In my own work with organisations, I have initiated counselling, leadership courses, mentoring, outplacement, dispute resolution, post-employment programs, moving to retirement training, relationship support and business development. None of those opportunities would have been possible without an attitude focused on learning, and adding value. The benefits to the Church become obvious after trust is established in these areas which leads to spiritual direction, worship, baptism, family support, funerals, marriage and the formation of communities within workplaces. The Catholic Church must do the work of engagement before respect can be conferred.

The placement of chaplains in workplaces is an important starting initiative. However, such a role requires a substantially different mindset and spirituality to other chaplaincies. This role may be widely misunderstood, may attract some opposition and will not naturally be seen as advantageous to the business. Recognition and appreciation must be earned by usefulness, value, and professionalism. No-one will care about your rich prayer life or worldly wisdom; your value will be judged on how much support, intelligence and effective tasks you complete.

The support systems for such chaplaincies must be developed by the individual chaplains. Personal mentoring and debriefing will not normally be available within a workplace. This requires self-motivated and experienced chaplains. Additionally, chaplains within workplaces are usually contracted, which signifies a role "of the company" but also "not of the company". This can be an unusual space to occupy, given that it requires loyalty to the workplace but sufficient independence to support workers in matters of confidentiality and privacy.

There is a noticeable tendency in some Catholic organisations to support potentially left leaning causes. It is important that Catholic initiatives within the workplace are free from social, political and commercial bias. Any perception of bias for or against one ethnic group or political party is unhelpful. This is one of the reasons Catholicism has failed to effectively connect to business, at least in its Australian context. The development of relationships and initiatives with the business community must be beyond agenda and political bias.

A stronger Catholic connection with business should be a central arm of the "New Evangelisation", but this will require a Catholic understanding in which our truth is placed within contexts that can be understood in a working environment and by people who have no historical connection to the Church. The current secular workplace offers significant opportunities for a Catholicism prepared to open itself to developing new ways of packaging the centrality of Christ in human life. Significantly, there now exists little "brand differentiation" between the Christian denominations. Younger managers may not be familiar with the inter-denominational rivalries of the past but will be concerned to hear of beneficial outcome for their companies. The "new evangelisation" to the workplace must be packaged within this context.

Catholic Expertise

Modern society is increasingly complex and intricate, particularly in social areas, ethical viewpoints, relationships between races and competing visions of national and regional futures.

Within many dioceses in Western nations, there are few opportunities for scholars, businessmen, bio-ethicists or concerned Catholics to analyse, discuss and present Catholic viewpoints in the light of fast changing societal events. The great difficulty for the Catholic Church is responding effectively to these developments. As a result it is often reacting to events and producing statements that are inadequately researched or merely offer excuses for past mistakes or poor behaviour. More seriously, the Church is frequently silent on matters that concern ordinary citizens: employment, commerce, business, education, family life, children, marriage and national and societal visions. These are all areas of life that require substantial analysis and research, leading to effective solutions, specifically based on a Catholic worldview and moral position.

There are a number of noticeable reasons why a predominantly clergy led church may be struggling to contend effectively with fast changing economic issues: wealth distribution, employment, remuneration, free trade, resources, interest rates, budgets, unionism and wider political strategies.

Seminary training concentrates on providing loving, effective and functioning priests and there is rightly no requirement for economic or commercial study. Nevertheless, as these issues become more prominent in the lives of Catholics throughout the world, the Church is increasingly being asked to provide direction and guidance in economic areas. No priest within a parochial situation will be trained to provide advice or guidance on such matters, yet many attempt to do so. The well-intentioned, self-taught amateur risks confusion, simplistic solutions or disaffected laity when the teachings of Christ are brought to bear on such issues without substantial knowledge or understanding.

The practical reality for the Church is that many of its parishes, agencies and diocesan voices resort to simplistic understandings and explanations concerning social justice or support for the poor, without any effective methodology on how to achieve such aims. Facts and figures, preparation, costs, required resources and the ability to sustain or drive a debate are often missing.

Currently in many Western nations there is no effective body that can intelligently and coherently produce resources, stimulate debate, provide regular articles to newspapers, journals, or the internet to support Catholics in their daily lives around such vital and sometimes confronting issues.

In particular, Australian Catholicism needs to consider the establishment of an economic peak-body think tank to provide information and resources around such matters and more importantly to form, lead and shape debate within the wider community that supports, explains and accentuates Catholic teaching and understanding in these areas.

It is no longer possible for the Church to remain wedded to understandings of economic matters that are not sufficiently developed and researched and unable to stand up to vigorous scrutiny now provided by many differing groups within our society. An inability or reluctance to change will see the important and vital voice of Catholicism increasingly forced from the public square.

Parish Life

Parish life, to an ever increasing extent, is placing great demands on parish priests and faithful laity. It can no longer be assumed that Catholics will make a significant effort to attend their local parish. Many will do so only for baptisms, weddings funerals, Christmas, Easter or out of duty for events associated with the local Catholic school attended by their children.

The lamentable reality is that most baptised and confirmed Catholics have no interest or desire to frequent their local parish. This is not a new situation in the West, but is one that has resulted in large numbers of defections to evangelical protestant denominations or more recently conversion to other faiths, notably Islam, Buddhism and new age philosophy. Clearly, the process of baptising and confirming younger Australians is not a guarantee of lifelong devotion to the faith or of its practical expression in future Mass attendance.

Catholicism cannot continue to be a wide open container at one end, yet one consisting of massive holes in its base!

Parish communities must devote a significant increase in their resources to the maintenance and support of those they already have, especially young families and singles under 25. These two groups are the building blocks of the future Church. Without their continued allegiance and nurture, the Church risks ongoing decline and eventual extinction.

It can be disheartening to see not only the absence of these demographic groups in many parishes but also the lack of awareness of the critical condition of many parish communities without these groups.

The parish community requires greater coordination around a series of fundamental actions, few of which are implemented correctly, maintained aggressively or used purposefully.

These urgent actions include a full list of each parishioner, relevant personal history, current workplace, telephone, email and facebook connections. All of this information can be acquired legally, professionally and without privacy concerns. Every gymnasium or sporting association obtains this information in order to communicate effectively with its members but most importantly to better understand the needs, hopes and dreams of its adherents. All sporting teams make intimate two-way conversation between coaches, supporters and sponsors a normal outcome of their networks. Almost all parishes fail to do this or see communication as a one-way outcome. A parish newsletter can still be maintained but offers nothing in terms of engagement, listening, dialogue or responding to expectations or concerns. Without these vehicles a parish is effectively blind and unfortunately risks suggesting to those who do attend that their views, attitudes, concerns or hopes are not central in the life of the parish. To complete these tasks effectively is a lot of work, but let us not complain that Mass attendance and Catholic loyalty is low, when we don't make these basic endeavours.

At base, successfully belonging to a parish community is centred on a few fundamental questions. Of highest importance in this membership paradigm is the question: Am I making progress? Parishioners must feel within themselves that the faith is working for them in their lives and that they understand more and more of its teachings. While duty is important, few people give much credibility to this aspect of life and are not likely to apply it to a Catholic allegiance when it occurs so rarely in other dimensions of life.

A willingness to stay part of a faithful community must consist of some dimensions of "success" (I am getting there) and some aspect of effective service, which feeds back into the notion that my faith is working.

Without this dimension of "making progress" people will cease to maintain parish membership. It is important that parish priests know their parishioners for this very reason – "making progress" is difficult to see, feel or understand in a faith context. It is the job of the priest to keep in touch with the hopes of his people. Every parishioner will be different and have different understandings of "getting there", yet failure to put in place individual markers of "getting better" will mean people will leave usually with the view that somehow "Catholicism didn't work for me".

A cardinal rule of faith development is simple. No people will leave your parish if they feel they are making progress. The context for this is that faith development is not a one-off event. Renewal, new growth and constant learning are essential in supporting initial allegiance to Christ.

Another important dimension of parish success is attendance. Attendance at Mass and parish events must be of value, in and of itself. Within the Catholic community coming to Mass must be part of lifestyle and a habit that has value in itself but which is connected to making progress in the faith. These two aspects intertwine together: if I make progress, I come to Mass; if I come to Mass I make progress.

Human beings are overwhelmingly creatures of habit. If I miss Mass for two Sundays, whatever the validity of the excuse, I am at risk of forming a new habit that subconsciously suggests that my life has not diminished because I failed to attend Mass; or indeed I can still call myself a good Catholic as I still attend more than many others. The risk in this thinking is that it assumes progress in the faith can still be made without the weekly "training dimension" of Mass attendance. Mass needs more value than "duty" or "learning more information" about the faith. Ironically, going to Mass is about furthering a relationship with a lover but love will be lost without time spent together; not through the "thrill of love" but through the "practice of habit". It is the habitual things that maintain the love over generations.

For a parish priest to understand the needs of his parishioners and how best to grow their love of Christ, he must be in "relationship" with them. His life is often the most concrete example for parishioners of how the faith can work in life and fulfil its purpose. If a parish priest is grumpy, isolated or unknown to his people, then how can he expect to make the faith "real"? If he does not share their food and know their stories, hopes and fears, how can he point the way? It is from a priest's relationship with parishioners that he can understand a journey, straighten a weakness, or suggest a new path. If a priest does not know his people, how will he even know if they are still coming?

There are a good number of things the parishes can do to strengthen relationships and help keep people developing their faith and service.

Central to this is "greeting teams", a number of parishioners who dedicate themselves to knowing and supporting other parishioners. This means talking to them, learning about their work, families and interests. If people are valued in this way the habit of attendance is easier to maintain. These "teams" also allow for constant updates on how the parish is travelling and provide feedback in a gentle way as to what might not be working. The parish priest cannot be the only individual taking the pulse of the parish. Local parishioners themselves must also undertake this role.

Additionally, parishes need to constantly check that outlined goals, objectives and mission statements are still being aimed for. Too many parishes present these, never to return to them. Concrete local examples of mission must be expressed, reached or modified.

Unfortunately, many parishes are unable to develop local goals or harness the skills and energy of the parishioners. In the first instance it may be necessary to instigate outside "resurgence teams" (www.theresurgence.org) to help in the development of parish models, youth groups, family support or most importantly local parish initiatives undertaken in a particular local style addressing local issues or concerns.

Subsidiarity is at the heart of Catholic philosophy. Importantly no two parishes are the same yet too many parishes still rely on diocesan agencies to do all the local lifting. Catholic parishes without local aims and initiatives risk disconnection from their communities and a consequent inability to speak to them. "We are what we do" is not a perfect philosophy but it may be the standard by which outsiders judge the local Catholic parish.

The value of local initiatives should not be underestimated in terms of energising parishioners, bonding communities and displaying "Catholicism in a nutshell" to those who do not yet know of Christ's life or teaching.

The tasks facing Catholicism within the Western world sometimes appear overwhelming. No doubt in every age Catholics have felt the same. Nevertheless, small steps are crucial. If I am an individual who must repay a loan of $100,000, a desperate visit to the racetrack is not the answer. Small gains are the way forward. Can I repay $100,000 next week? No! But I can repay $500 and so the task of financial independence has begun. Jesus suggested something similar in his parable of the mustard seed:

> What is the Kingdom of God like, and to what shall I compare it? It is like a mustard seed which a man took and

threw into his own garden and it grew and became a tree and the birds of the air nested in its branches (Luke 13:18-19).

Yes, the challenges facing the Church are enormous and exhausting. Nevertheless, it is also true that the opportunities to bring about Christ's purpose in our world are far more spirited and dynamic.

www.ingramcontent.com/pod-product-compliance
Lightning Source LLC
Chambersburg PA
CBHW062012180426
43199CB00034B/2472